enjoy!

ISBN 13: 978-1-63489-162-2

LIBRARY OF CONGRESS CATALOG NUMBER: 2018954424
PRINTED IN CANADA
FIRST PRINTING: 2018
22 21 20 19 18   5 4 3 2 1
COVER AND INTERIOR DESIGN BY KAYLA ADAMS

WISE INK CREATIVE PUBLISHING
807 BROADWAY ST. NE, SUITE 46
MINNEAPOLIS, MN 55413
WISEINK.COM

TO ORDER, VISIT ITASCABOOKS.COM OR CALL 1-800-901-3480.
RESELLER DISCOUNTS AVAILABLE.

- - - - - - - - - -

TREASURED TIMES

Seasonal Recipes *and*
Unique Traditions *to* Savor Together

- - - - - - - - - -

WRITTEN BY
JARYN McGRATH

STYLED BY
THE SHIFT CREATIVE

in loving memory of

MY SISTER JENNY

ONE OF MY FAVORITE MEMORIES WITH YOU IS
WHEN WE USED TO SNEAK CANDY IN THE BATHTUB
AS LITTLE GIRLS, HIDING WRAPPERS BEHIND THE
SHAMPOO BOTTLES, THINKING THAT MOM WOULD
NEVER FIND THEM. THANK YOU FOR GIVING ME
THE COUNTLESS MOMENTS WITH YOU THAT I WILL
TREASURE FOREVER.

pumpkin black
bean soup

CONTENTS

introduction

A few years ago, my friend Amy Carlin told me that I needed to write a book about the different activities and traditions that I implement with my family. She had witnessed us handing out balloons and flowers to various people during our Be Thoughtful Thursdays in the Summertime; she heard teachers talking about the Appreciation Brunch that we hold at our house every January for the teachers, coaches, and church leaders who have made an impact in our children's lives; and she saw me continually serving around the school and community. I responded, "Doesn't everyone do things like this?" I was lucky enough to be raised by a mother whose ultimate goal has always been family togetherness and service in the community. Many of you actually have these same goals and graciously implement them, but some of you may be looking for some new, unique ideas to apply with your families.

Treasured Times is written for anyone seeking to develop lasting connections with the ones they love. As we spend time and have meaningful experiences with family members, close friends, and loved ones, we gain the sense of security and acceptance that we all crave. I have seen it with my own children. Because they have support at home, they are growing into confident, caring, and strong individuals. They are also being raised in an accepting community that reinforces their growth. When our children face hard times, which we all do, I can only hope that they will cling to these traditions to get them through.

In this book, each chapter focuses on a month of the year. I emphasize one big event per chapter, but I include a page of extras at the end of each chapter with some additional fun and simple ideas. The pages are filled with gorgeous photographs, delicious recipes, and various how-to guides.

Some chapters focus on merely having fun and making memories as a family, which I find important and rewarding. Some examples to look for are the Fondue Party in February, the Talent Show in March, the Solstice Kick-Off in June, and the Concerts at the Park in July. Other chapters, such as the Appreciation Brunch in January, Serving the Homeless in November, and the Sugar Cookie Decorating Kits in December, focus on serving others and making a difference in our community. Then I have the chapters that focus on helping our children find and make spiritual connections on a much higher level, like An Evening in Jerusalem in April and School Year's Eve in August.

Although the photographs on these pages are breathtakingly beautiful, they are styled shots. They are definitely not representative of our real everyday life. I hired an amazing team, The Shift Creative, to help me make this book aesthetically pleasing, and they went above and beyond my expectations. On a normal year, our Fondue Party is a little more casual, with various foods thrown in bowls, along with our ugly, oily fondue pot that we've had for over fifteen years. The reason I point these things out is so that you don't get discouraged when your newfound traditions don't look as flawless as the ones on these pages. I hope that some of these ideas will become yearly traditions for you, but I also understand that we lead busy lives, and not all of these events can happen every year. Aim for easy. Aim for mellow. Aim for the true feelings that emerge when you are with the ones you love most.

I recently read *Present Over Perfect: Leaving Behind Frantic for a Simpler, More Soulful Way of Living* by Shauna Niequist and *Chasing Slow: Courage to Journey off the Beaten Path* by Erin Loechner. These pieces are eloquent reminders that we must search for beauty in an imperfect, present, and slow lifestyle. My goal is that you will use my ideas with a deliberate choice to keep them imperfect, present, and slow. Enjoy every moment as the people you love dip their fingers in chocolate fondue in February. Savor the peace as you carefully lather your children's feet in April. And giggle uncontrollably as your boyfriend or spouse chases you during a kickball game in June. Cherish every moment, because these are our treasured times.

january

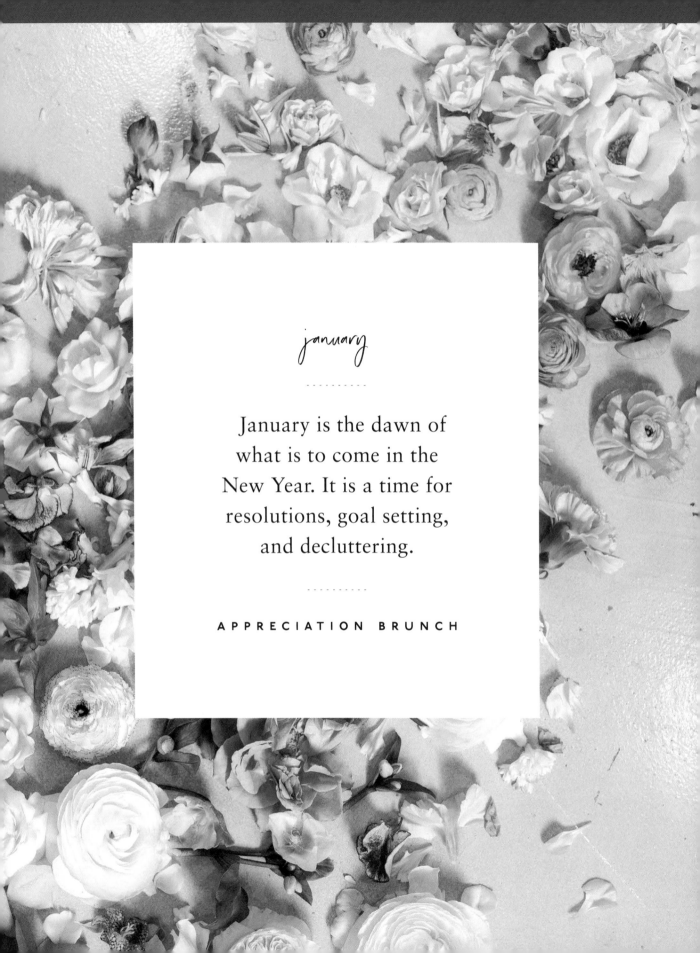

january

· · · · · · · · · · ·

January is the dawn of
what is to come in the
New Year. It is a time for
resolutions, goal setting,
and decluttering.

· · · · · · · · · · ·

APPRECIATION BRUNCH

January's APPRECIATION BRUNCH

January is the dawn of all that is to come in the New Year. It is a time for resolutions, goal setting, and decluttering. For me, it is a month of simplicity. After the holiday decorations are packed away, the tinsel is cleaned up, the pine needles are vacuumed, and the bellies are bulging, I am in dire need of a cleanse: physical, spiritual, emotional, and mental. January is a much-needed refresher. As a family, we meet together and declare our resolutions, put them to paper with deep, dark ink and a signature, and display them to remind us of our goals throughout the year.

One of our recurring family goals is to give back to the community that we are a part of, the community that selflessly gives to us every single day. A way that our family has decided to do this is to host an Appreciation Brunch every January for all of the many people who have made a difference in our children's lives over the past year.

The children compile lists of school-teachers, coaches, music teachers, and leaders in our church that have influenced them over the past year. Then they send out invitations. Once we get the final guest count, we make nametags, we create a menu, and the kids write thank-you cards to all the attendees. Dressed in their Sunday best, the kids greet guests by taking their coats and showing them to their seats around flower-filled tables.

Throughout the brunch, the children deliver their handwritten cards and clear away plates as needed. We have held this brunch for the past five years, and we usually have about thirty people come.

The great thing about this tradition is that it is extremely versatile. If you'd like to adopt it on a much smaller scale, your children can show appreciation to your favorite babysitters or a nanny who cares for them, and you can have a more intimate brunch. Your family can show gratitude to a neighbor who keeps an eye on your house while you are out of town or to special friends who offer to carpool your kids to and from school. If you do not have children, you can throw an Appreciation Brunch for your closest friends or coworkers who always have your back. It is a great way to show people how grateful you are!

As the brunch comes to an end and the guests begin to file out, Dylan and I are always awed by the community of people who come together to bless our lives. We reflect on the numerous individuals who have such a positive and powerful influence on our children, and we conclude that it really does take a village to raise a child.

BRUNCH MENU

CROISSANTS

Chocolate, almond, or plain croissants found in the freezer section of Trader Joe's that you lay out to rise overnight and that leave the most wonderful aroma in your kitchen the next morning

VARIETY OF QUICHES

Ham and cheese; vegetarian; and gluten-free chicken and artichoke (I ordered these ahead of time from one of our local favorites, Pannikin Coffee and Tea)

COFFEE CAKE

Ordered ahead of time from Pannikin Coffee and Tea

FRESH-SQUEEZED ORANGE JUICE

MINI YOGURT PARFAITS WITH GRANOLA AND BERRIES

FRESH FRUIT

HOMEMADE CINNAMON ROLLS

See recipe on page 12

"

We reflect on the numerous individuals who have such a positive and powerful influence on our children, and we conclude that it really does take a village to raise a child.

"

JESSICA'S CINNAMON ROLLS

MAKES 24 ROLLS

My sister Jessica is an amazing baker. She brings butter-laden cakes and pies and cookies to every occasion, and we all drool. Her homemade cinnamon rolls are a mainstay on Christmas morning, and they are showstoppers at our Appreciation Brunch every year. We took a poll one year as to which flavor guests preferred: cinnamon or orange. Most adults preferred orange, while the children swooned over the cinnamon. I like both, of course.

INGREDIENTS

FOR THE DOUGH:

- 2 cups very warm water
- 2 tablespoons yeast
- I cup plus 2 tablespoons sugar
- I cup melted butter, cooled
- 6 beaten eggs
- I½ teaspoons salt
- 8½ cups plus ½ cup unbleached, all-purpose flour

FOR THE FILLING:

- ¾ cup softened butter
- I cup sugar
- cinnamon to your liking (be generous)

FOR THE FROSTING:

- ½ cup butter
- 4½ cups powdered sugar
- I teaspoon vanilla extract
- ¼ cup (or more) heavy cream

DIRECTIONS

1. Put water, yeast, and 2 tablespoons sugar in a mixer bowl fitted with a dough hook. Mix and let foam for a few minutes.
2. Add cooled butter; mix.
3. Add remaining sugar and eggs; mix.
4. Add salt and 4 cups flour; combine.
5. Add 4½ cups flour (save remaining ½ cup flour for rolling out).
6. Mix.
7. Pour dough into a large greased bowl and cover with a kitchen towel. Let rise 2–4 hours, until double.
8. Pour dough out onto floured surface. Roll into a rectangle about 13 by 18 inches. Spread softened butter on top; sprinkle with sugar and as much cinnamon as you like. Roll up the longer side of the dough (use a bench scraper to help). Cut into 24 even cinnamon rolls. Place in greased pan (preferably 13 by 18 inches and 2 inches deep). Cover and let rise again, 1–2 hours.
9. Bake at 350 degrees for 25 minutes on bottom rack.
10. Mix frosting ingredients, adding enough cream to make a nice consistency for spreading. Frost warm cinnamon rolls.
11. For orange rolls, use orange zest instead of cinnamon in the rolls and orange juice in place of the heavy cream for the frosting.

january

"Alone we can
do so little;
together we can
do so much."

HELEN KELLER

HERE ARE A FEW OTHER FAVORITE THINGS WE DO IN JANUARY

NEW YEAR'S RESOLUTIONS

Sit down together as a family and write out your resolutions for the New Year.

BOOK READING PARTY

Host a book reading party for your children and their friends. Invite them to bring pillows, stuffed animals, and all of their favorite books for a cozy afternoon. Serve hot chocolate and delicious snacks.

CREATE A SANCTUARY

Create a sanctuary in a quiet space of your home where you and your children can go to recharge. Ours is in a small nook of our master bedroom, and in it we have a fluffy white blanket, journals to write in, poetry books, candles, a diffuser with essential oils, air plants, and a little bit of Shakespeare—all atop a bamboo garment rack.

WHOLE LIVING CLEANSE

Do Martha Stewart's Whole Living Action Plan. After the holidays, my body always needs a good cleanse. I follow the Whole Living Action Plan for the first three weeks of January every year.

CAPSULE WARDROBE

Look into starting a capsule wardrobe. I began mine three years ago, and it has simplified my life and changed my outlook on clothing. A great resource for more information is the blog *Unfancy* by Caroline Rector.

february

february

· · · · · · · · · ·

What better way to
celebrate this sizzling love
that Dylan and I have than
to gather our children
around our fondue pot and
celebrate our love with
them a few days before
Valentine's Day every year?

· · · · · · · · · ·

VALENTINE
FONDUE PARTY

february's VALENTINE FONDUE PARTY

I navigated the ins and outs of my new fondue pot when I finally got a place of my own during my sophomore year of college. I was out of the dorms and living life with Stephanie, Megan, and Heather as my roommates in Arlington Heights. Stephanie didn't have much of an interest in cooking at the time, and Megan was overloaded with schoolwork. Heather and I were definitely planners. She and I would sit together on Sundays and plan out our meals for the week. We scoured cookbooks, made grocery lists, and chose the particular nights we would all sit down to eat together. This is where my love of meal planning all began. As long as Stephanie and Megan didn't mind pitching in money for food, Heather and I cooked dinner for us all. We especially loved inviting (handsome) single male friends over to taste it all.

There were definitely a few learning experiences along the way, like serving what Jonathon liked to call "pink chicken" (which was really chicken not cooked completely through), making quesadillas that seemed a little off and then realizing we accidentally bought imitation shredded cheese (but it was so cheap!), and whacking chicken paillards with mallets until Chandler finally ended up confiscating the mallets and took over the kitchen for the rest of the night, making dinner for us all. That kitchen at Arlington Heights was where I learned how to make my children's absolute favorite meal: chicken pillows. Heather brought the recipe from home to share with me. We gabbed about boys, schoolwork, and the snowstorm rolling in as we rolled these creamy, comforting dumplings in melted butter and seasoned breadcrumbs.

College days were some of the best times.

I had a bit of a crush on Jack Peterson for quite some time, but it was the kind of thing that I knew would never go anywhere. For one thing, I had just broken up with Tom. For another, Jack was five years older than me. I met Jack while taking a college ice skating class with my girlfriends.

At first, I thought Jack was a little odd, being the only man in a figure skating class of girls when all of the other guys were speeding around the next rink over with their hockey sticks in hand. But then I realized how clever

> *While the tempura sizzles in the oil, we retell our love story to our children.*

he was, being the only man amongst all of these young single women . . . brilliant!

Jack was mature, handsome, and off-limits. At first, I pretended that I didn't notice him. I would skate around the rink with my waist-long dark hair flowing behind me. As the semester rolled on, I gained a little more courage every time I saw him, flirting my way around. I couldn't believe it when one day he finally skated up beside me and took a few laps by my side. He asked where I was from and informed me that he was from Chicago. He couldn't put his finger on what nationality I was, so I kept him guessing: Latin? Indian? Persian? I wish I could say that I was completely at ease as we skated alongside each other. But I was trembling inside, and it took every clenched muscle in my body to keep me from toppling over on the smooth, glistening ice.

I don't remember how, but at some point in the semester, I got enough courage to ask him over to our condo for a fondue dinner. He obliged but warned me that he would have to rush off to a highly attended Sunday devotional where he would be taking photos for our college newspaper. That was fine by me, especially since I'd just gotten a call from this new guy, Dylan, asking me if I was going to the Sunday devotional that night. He was wondering if I wanted to sit by him. This Dylan was very handsome, and he and I had recently ended up in my car on a road trip to California with two of my girlfriends. I didn't think much would come of the whole thing, but I could tell that Dylan was a little interested when he kept stopping by my place unannounced. He didn't know about this infatuation with Jack or of the other guys buzzing around in my life.

The devotional was amazing. I don't remember now what the presenter said, but I do remember the feeling that I had while I sat by Dylan. I glanced down a few times to where Jack was sitting with his huge-lensed Nikon, and I realized that he was just another guy. I realized that I was a lucky girl to be sitting by this tanned, dark-haired, chiseled guy who didn't play games and was very straightforward about the way he felt for me. I leaned over to him during the devotional and questioned in his ear if he'd like to come over for some leftover tempura fondue that my roommates and I didn't get a chance to finish before the devotional.

(The same fondue that I shared with Jack just hours before.)

(I know. I'm a tramp.)

With complete ease, Dylan joined my roommates and me around the fondue pot that night coating the chicken, zucchini, onions, and broccoli with tempura batter, asking questions while the food sizzled in the bubbling oil. I felt something inside me sizzling and bubbling—and, just like that, Jack became a wisp of a memory.

So what better way to celebrate this sizzling love that Dylan and I have than to gather our children around our fondue pot (the same one we used in college) and celebrate our love with them a few days before Valentine's Day every year? We enjoy this elegant meal on Sunday, adorning the table with flickering candles, sparkling drinks, and delicious food. While the tempura sizzles in the oil, we retell our love story to our children.

TEMPURA BATTER

INGREDIENTS

- 2¼ cups flour
- 1½ teaspoons salt
- 1½ teaspoons pepper
- 3 tablespoons vegetable oil
- 3 egg yolks
- 1½ cups vegetable stock

DIRECTIONS

1. Combine flour, salt, and pepper in a mixing bowl.
2. Add oil, egg yolks, and vegetable stock; stir until smooth.
3. Dredge various foods in batter and fry in hot oil until crispy.

OUR FAVORITE FOODS TO DRENCH IN TEMPURA

- chunks of mozzarella cheese
- avocado
- onion
- chicken
- zucchini
- yellow squash
- sweet potato
- broccoli
- Lit'l Smokies cocktail links (they end up tasting like mini corn dogs)
- mushrooms

SAUCES

- soy sauce
- gyoza sauce from Trader Joe's
- sweet chili sauce from Trader Joe's

ALMOND SHORTBREAD COOKIES

These buttery, crumbly shortbread cookies have the perfect hint of almond extract in the glaze that sets them apart from other varieties. They become extra rich and delicious when dunked in your chocolate fondue.

INGREDIENTS

- 1½ cups butter, at room temperature
- 1 cup granulated sugar
- 1 teaspoon vanilla extract
- 3 teaspoons almond extract
- 3½ cups all-purpose flour
- ¼ teaspoon kosher salt
- 1½ cups chopped almonds (optional)
- 1 cup powdered sugar

DIRECTIONS

1. Preheat the oven to 350 degrees.
2. Combine the butter and sugar in the bowl of an electric mixer.
3. Add vanilla and 1 teaspoon almond extract.
4. Add flour and salt; mix well.
5. Mix in the almonds on low speed until the dough comes together (I have made the cookies without the almonds and they taste just as wonderful). Dump onto a floured surface and shape into a flat disk.
6. Wrap in plastic and chill for 30 minutes.
7. Roll the dough ½-inch thick, and use fluted cookie cutters to make shapes.
8. Place cookies on an ungreased baking sheet.
9. Bake for 20–25 minutes. I take mine out of the oven before they get cooked too much to ensure a soft crunch.

FOR THE ALMOND GLAZE:

1. With a fork, mix together 1 cup powdered sugar, 4 teaspoons water, and 2 teaspoons almond extract to make the glaze for the cookies.
2. When the cookies are not quite cooled all the way, drizzle the almond glaze on with a spoon.

february

· · · · · · · · · ·

"All you need is love. But a little chocolate now and then doesn't hurt."

· · · · · · · · · ·

CHARLES SCHULZ

recipe three

CHOCOLATE FONDUE

I have found chocolate to be a bit tricky in our fondue pot. Since I can't regulate the heat as well as I can over a gas stove, it tends to burn and get chalky quite easily. If you have this problem too, heat your chocolate* in a double boiler until silky smooth (you may add a touch of cream), and then transfer to the fondue pot on the lowest heat setting to keep warm. If you don't want to try the double-boiler method and would like to heat your chocolate in the fondue pot, the best option is to buy melting chocolate wafers that are specifically designed for dipping.

SWEETS TO DIP IN CHOCOLATE FONDUE

- strawberries
- bananas
- peaches
- nectarines
- raspberries
- marshmallows
- doughnut holes
- brownie bites
- cream puffs
- homemade shortbread cookies
- pretzels

DOUBLE BOILER HOW-TO

1. Fill a medium pot about ¼ full with water and bring to a boil.
2. Reduce to a simmer and fit a glass bowl on top of the pot. There should be a couple of inches between the water and the glass bowl.
3. Pour chocolate into glass bowl and stir until melted through. Remove from heat.

My favorite chocolates to use are the semi-sweet chocolate chips from See's Candies. They are sold in a 1-lb bag. Dylan is a white chocolate fan, so for him I use Ghirardelli's white chocolate wafers.

HERE ARE A FEW OTHER FAVORITE THINGS WE DO IN FEBRUARY

HEARTS ALL AROUND

Use heart-shaped cookie cutters of all sizes to make every meal a love fest! Use them on toast, apples, scones, sandwiches, brownies, homemade croutons, and carrots in your homemade chicken noodle soup recipe. You've got the idea!

VALENTINE SOCK HOP

Invite all of your kids' friends over for an old-fashioned Valentine sock hop. Serve heart-shaped grilled cheese sandwiches, french fries, and strawberry milkshakes or root beer floats.

HEART ATTACKS

Give someone a "heart attack"! Write love notes on heart-shaped cutouts and tape to wooden skewers, making them look like big lollipops. Sneak over to your best friend's house (or lover's, or neighbor's), and poke them into the grass all over the front yard.

PRESIDENTS' DAY

With your children, celebrate Presidents' Day by building log cabins out of pretzels, peanut butter, and graham crackers.

CREATE A MIXED VINYL RECORD

For your mod lover, create a vinyl record with your choice of love songs to give to him or her on Valentine's Day. (Or you can burn a CD . . . but a record is just so cool!) Go to vinylify.com for more details.

march

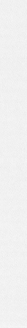

march

· · · · · · · · ·

This is a time for the kids to shine amongst each other and share with us their varying talents.

· · · · · · · · ·

FAMILY TALENT
SHOW

march's FAMILY TALENT SHOW

All of the grandchildren pull out their best costumes, tune up their instruments, set the stage, dust off the microphone, and pass out programs for our annual family talent show.

This is a time for the kids to shine amongst each other and share with us their varying talents. From piano and guitar solos to choreographed dances to comedy acts to Lego building, it is definitely an evening to remember—an *America's Got Talent* right in our own backyard.

For my mom's birthday in March every year, she asks the grandchildren to share a talent as a gift to her. You can definitely start a talent show any time of the year, though. Our kids also perform for my dad during Christmastime, but another great idea would be to include a talent show in your next family reunion.

Now, at events like these, we've always got to have good food! My mom adores ravioli, and we usually have a full-blown pasta, garlic bread, and salad spread for the occasion. Since I am featuring my favorite pasta and garlic bread recipe in the August chapter of this book, I am going to suggest a grilled cheese bar—another one of our favorite foods! A grilled cheese bar is great for a crowd, and it pleases the pickiest of eaters since you get to choose your own ingredients.

Just recently, I picked up some family videos from Costco that I had transferred from mini DVR tapes to DVDs. Dylan, the kids, and I sprawled across our couches with blankets and filled a Sunday afternoon catching up on the good ol' times. Seven was so little, and he had the cutest voice. We were *those* parents, the ones who spent every minute of every day videotaping their child's every move. *Oh, he just picked up a ball! Oh, he just picked his nose! He's so cute, he just sneezed!*

> "Time passes ever so quickly, and in moments like the Annual Family Talent Show, we slow down and truly savor our time together.

Those were the days.

One of the videos had a tape of our family talent show from 2008 when we performed for my mom in Hawaii, adorned with hula skirts and coconut shells. These kids have grown so much since then—especially Zander and Trazer, the oldest of the grandchildren, who used to take naps with me as babies and now have huge thighs and are out of high school.

Time passes by ever so quickly, and in moments like the Annual Family Talent Show, we slow down and truly savor our time together. When I glance over at my mom in March or my dad in December, I see their faces beaming in awe of who their grandchildren have become.

grocery list

BUILD-YOUR-OWN
GRILLED CHEESE BAR

VARIETY OF BREADS

- sourdough
- whole wheat
- white
- roasted garlic
- rosemary
- asiago
- gluten-free
- squaw
- sweet Hawaiian

VARIETY OF CHEESES

- cheddar
- american
- brie
- gouda
- mozzarella
- pepper jack
- swiss

GARNISHES

- salt and pepper
- rosemary
- basil
- olive oil
- honey
- cinnamon

VARIETY OF FILLINGS

- apples
- pears
- tomatoes
- grilled or pickled onions
- avocados
- roasted bell peppers
- basil
- pesto (see Jaryn's Pesto recipe in May)
- spinach
- bacon
- jams or chutneys
- brown sugar

VARIETY OF SPREADS FOR THE OUTSIDE

- butter
- mayonnaise
- crème fraîche
- Clearman's Spread
- olive oil
- mixture of parmesan and butter

march

· · · · · · · · · ·

"The family is one of
nature's masterpieces."

· · · · · · · · · ·

GEORGE SANTAYANA

HERE ARE A FEW OTHER FAVORITE THINGS WE DO IN MARCH

ST. PATRICK'S DAY
Enjoy an Irish feast on St. Patrick's Day. Prepare corned beef and cabbage, Irish soda bread, and shamrock sugar cookies.

CATCH A LEPRECHAUN!
Make leprechaun traps out of shoeboxes, paint, gold glitter, and other craft supplies with your children.

GARDENING
Start a garden, even if it's just a few pots of herbs on the back porch.

MAKE FLOWER CROWNS
Get outside on a beautiful spring day and collect flowers to make flower crowns.

MARCH MADNESS
If you're a sports fan, join in on the action of March Madness and support your favorite college basketball team.

april

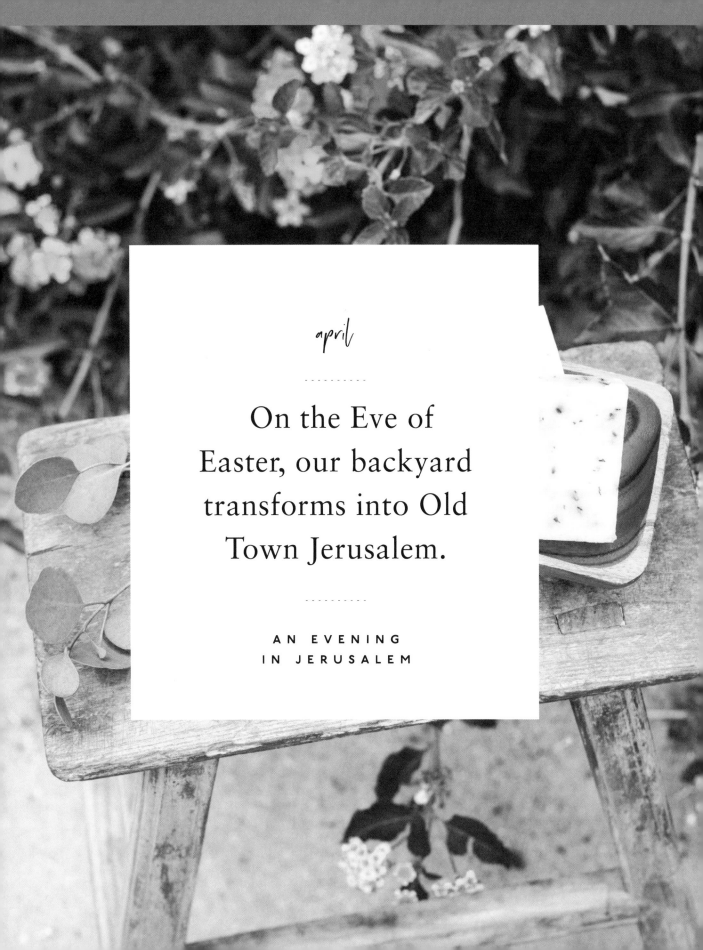

april

- - - - - - - - - -

On the Eve of Easter, our backyard transforms into Old Town Jerusalem.

- - - - - - - - - -

AN EVENING
IN JERUSALEM

april's EVENING IN JERUSALEM

As a mother of four children, I put a lot of pressure on myself in how I raise my kids. I want them to be happy, find joy in life, be grateful for everything, make sure to always remember to say please and thank you, include everyone, get good grades, be respectful to their teachers, never hit or yell at each other, remember what a great mom I was when they are older, avoid cavities, keep their music teacher Lyle from telling them they need to practice more, listen the first time I ask them to do something, do all of their chores every day, put only nutritious food into their mouths, and keep God and Jesus Christ at the center of their lives. Is that too much to ask?

All joking aside, my main goal as a mother is to raise children who love the Lord. That is why this tradition is special to me. It gives our family a chance to remember what is really important, especially during a season filled with Cadbury Eggs, chocolate bunnies, and Peeps galore.

On the eve of Easter, our backyard transforms into Old Town Jerusalem. Muslin, olive wood serving platters, and oil lamps are scattered about. Dylan and I shuffle the low-seated kid table from the craft room to our outside patio and lay out spreads of flatbreads with hummus and goat cheese and tapenade, clusters of plump deep purple grapes, hearty bowls of lentil soup, olives, and intensely flavored sparkling pomegranate juice. We buy all these items at the store, making it easy for me to focus on the purpose of this sacred tradition. Instead of bustling around the kitchen like I normally do, I try to keep a sense of peacefulness in our home leading up to our special evening. I give myself permission to make it an easy night by not cooking all day, and I give myself permission to not feel guilty about not making a homemade meal. The goal of this evening is to root our children's

> **" *. . . my main goal as a mother is to raise children who love the Lord. That is why this tradition is special to me. It gives our family a chance to remember what is really important . . .* **

faith in a deep, earthy soil. Dylan and I invite them outside for the most sacred part of the evening—getting their feet washed. As we remove the shoes from their feet, we talk of Jesus, of His love for His disciples, and of His love for them.

We then pour warm water over their feet and talk of the dirty, dusty roads of Jerusalem that Jesus and His disciples walked on in mere straps of leather around their rough feet. Slowly lathering in soap, we speak of the cleansing power of Christ's Atonement. And then we massage oils into their perfect, tiny feet before we join together sitting on pillows around the low table for our Evening in Jerusalem. The mood is dim, with oil lanterns

flickering and casting dancing shadows about. It is somber and peaceful, and the only sounds to be heard are Johann Sebastian Bach's *Easter Oratorio* quietly humming in the background and the reverent voices of our usually loud children.

Grasping onto every last ounce of this emotional night, we come to terms that it must end and that the kids will be excited about something completely different on the upcoming Easter morning. As dishes are cleared and flames are snuffed, my soul grins at the lessons Dylan and I teach our children. We hope this is what they will remember forever. Moments like these.

grocery list

JERUSALEM FEAST

The great thing is that all of these items can be found at your local

grocery store. I get everything from Trader Joe's.

- sparkling pomegranate juice
- plump grapes
- fresh figs
- sliced cucumbers
- raw honey
- hummus
- lentil soup
- flatbreads
- pita chips or other crackers
- goat cheese
- feta cheese
- tabbouleh
- pistachios
- olives
- dates

INNER STRENGTH MASSAGE OIL

To create a rich and earthy massage oil that will help increase spirituality, follow the instructions below. This oil is a perfect indulgence for this special evening with your children. It will uplift and balance moods and bring a sense of peace to the overall ambience of the night.

YOU WILL NEED:

- 4-ounce amber glass bottle with glass dropper
- 2 tablespoons dried organic rosebuds
- 3 ounces sweet almond oil
- 7 drops frankincense essential oil
- 2 drops bergamot essential oil
- 2 drops lemon essential oil

DIRECTIONS

1. Carefully drop rosebuds into glass bottle.
2. Pour sweet almond oil into bottle, and drop essential oils in.
3. Replace glass dropper cap and slowly swirl bottle to combine all oils.

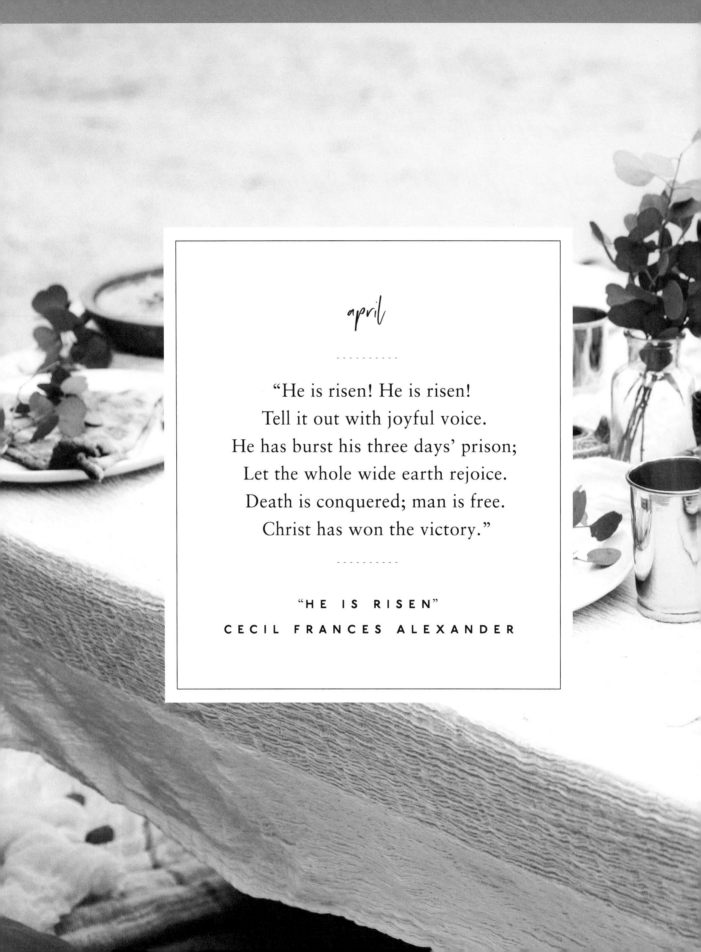

april

· · · · · · · · · ·

"He is risen! He is risen!
Tell it out with joyful voice.
He has burst his three days' prison;
Let the whole wide earth rejoice.
Death is conquered; man is free.
Christ has won the victory."

· · · · · · · · · ·

"HE IS RISEN"
CECIL FRANCES ALEXANDER

HERE ARE A FEW OTHER FAVORITE THINGS WE DO IN APRIL

HOST AN EGG LAUNCH

Break up into teams and wrap uncooked eggs in an assortment of recycled media: bubble wrap, toilet paper rolls, newspaper, egg cartons, tissue boxes, packing tape, and anything else you can find. Launch each team's package off a balcony to see which egg survives unscathed. Award prizes to the winning teams.

CELEBRATE EARTH DAY

Celebrate Earth Day in April by vowing not to use electricity in your home the entire day. In preparation, set reminders out the night before. Our kids run around the house putting sticky notes marked with Xs on every light switch and appliance. This means no toaster, no hair dryer, no television, no blender, no washing machine, no lights . . . you get the idea! This makes for a romantic evening dinner by candlelight, and a cozy bedtime story with headlamps and lanterns. A big bonus is that you get the day off from doing laundry!

CANDLE-MAKING

With your children, roll sheets of beeswax honeycomb around long cotton wicks to make candles for your Evening in Jerusalem or for your energy-efficient Earth Day endeavors.

SPRING NATURE HIKE

Go on a spring nature hike and pick wildflowers for your April celebrations.

SPRAY PAINT EGGS

Spray paint hollowed-out eggs, break off the top quarter, and fill with tiny succulents or the wildflowers you picked on your spring nature hike.

may

may

Something about enjoying an elegant tea once in a while brings out the femininity in me.

MOTHER'S DAY TEA

may's MOTHER'S DAY TEA

In between my freshman and sophomore years of college, I came home for the summer to work at The Tea House on Los Rios in the historic town that I grew up in, San Juan Capistrano, California. It was a quaint and perfect little teahouse nestled behind train tracks, where the owners cut fresh roses every day to adorn tables, where you could sift through an array of colorful hats to wear for your afternoon tea, and where hot heart-shaped scones emerged from the oven on the regular. I may or may not have eaten a scone dripping with their in-house early California cream on my lunch break every single day.

I returned again when my mom and sisters threw me a girly baby shower to celebrate the coming of our first daughter, Melrose. I have been back many times since: with my nana, with a group of girlfriends for a Mother's Day brunch, and with my own daughters and their friends. Something about enjoying an elegant tea once in a while brings out the femininity in me.

Since I enjoy an elegant tea so much, I figured that others might too. I began selling a mother-daughter tea party at our elementary school's auction every year. I open it up to four mothers with their four daughters and make it special with an assortment of herbal teas, pink lemonade, homemade scones, sandwiches, salad, and my favorite lemon bars. It is so rewarding to witness the moms and daughters chitchatting with each other in their flowery dresses while enjoying a nice afternoon away from soccer games, swim meets, dance competitions, and the other variables that busy our Saturday afternoon schedules.

After selling this tea party year after year at our school auction, I began to wonder why I didn't implement this tradition with the beautiful women who have made an impact in my own life. So I invited my nana, my mom, my mother-in-law, my sisters, my sisters-in-law, and my stepsister for an afternoon to catch up with each other and nourish the connections that we have. My sister-in-law and stepsister flew in for the occasion from Utah and Texas, respectively, and we all spent the afternoon in good company, in the beautiful setting of a local nursery, Barrels and Branches. We used my great-great-grandmother's intricately detailed china that has been passed down to me, complete with dishes, salad bowls, platters, teacups, and saucers. What a great reminder of where we came from!

As we sat together slowly enjoying our cups of hot herbal tea, I contemplated the powerful women I have in my life who have taught me how to learn, how to be brave, how to serve, how to be compassionate, how to forgive, and most importantly, how to love God.

recipe one

CUCUMBER SANDWICHES

INGREDIENTS

- white bread
- whipped cream cheese
- English cucumber, sliced thin
- fresh dill

DIRECTIONS

1. Cut as many rounds as you like of white bread with a circle-shaped cookie cutter.
2. Spread with cream cheese.
3. Top each with one cucumber slice.
4. Garnish with dill.

LINDSAY'S TOMATO, BASIL, AND HAVARTI SANDWICHES

INGREDIENTS

- 1 fresh baguette
- 8 slices havarti
- 3 tomatoes, sliced thin
- 6–8 basil leaves
- salt and pepper to taste

PESTO SPREAD:

- 2 tablespoons mayonnaise
- 1 tablespoon Jaryn's Pesto (or store-bought)
- squeeze of lemon

DIRECTIONS

FOR THE PESTO SPREAD:

1. Mix together mayonnaise, pesto, and lemon to make a yummy spread.

FOR THE SANDWICHES:

1. Slice the baguette lengthwise, but keep one side connected.
2. Slather with pesto spread.
3. Layer cheese, then tomato, then basil on bread.
4. Season with salt and pepper.

recipe three

JARYN'S PESTO

INGREDIENTS

- 3 tablespoons pine nuts, toasted
- 2 cups fresh basil, rinsed and patted dry
- ¾ cup parmesan cheese
- 2 cloves garlic
- 2 tablespoons butter
- ⅔ cup olive oil
- ½ teaspoon salt
- dash of pepper

DIRECTIONS

1. Put all ingredients in a food processor or blender, and blend until smooth.
2. Refrigerate until ready to serve.
3. If freezing, drizzle oil on top to prevent browning and store in freezer for up to three months.

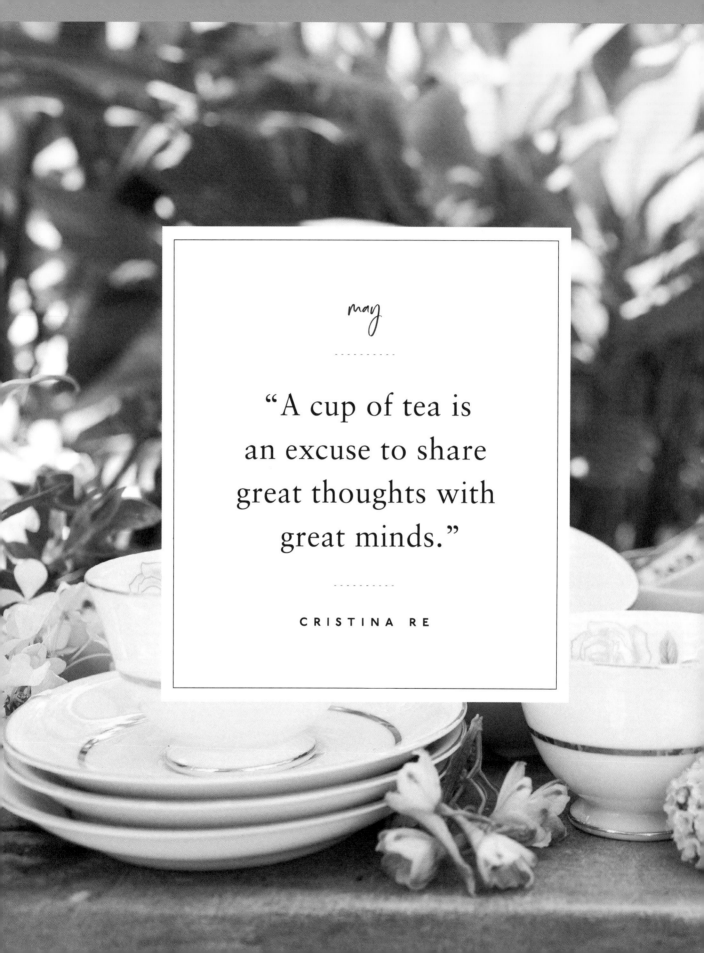

may

- - - - - - - - - -

"A cup of tea is
an excuse to share
great thoughts with
great minds."

- - - - - - - - - -

CRISTINA RE

recipe four

LEMON BARS

The first time I ever took a bite into a lemon bar was at Cynthia's Bakery in San Juan Capistrano. I was a little thing, probably only five years old, but it forever changed my life. My mom and sister Jenny were there to witness this moment, and they both drool over lemon bars as much as I do. Actually, our whole family does. One day years later, when that cute little bakery closed its doors, I experimented alone in the kitchen with a recipe I found in one of my childhood books, *Winnie-the-Pooh's Teatime Cookbook*. What came about were some of the best lemon bars I have ever tasted, and I still use the recipe to this day.

INGREDIENTS

FOR THE CRUST:

- 1 cup butter
- ½ cup powdered sugar
- 2 cups flour

FOR THE FILLING:

- 4 eggs
- ½ teaspoon lemon zest
- ½ teaspoon baking powder
- ⅓ cup fresh lemon juice
- ¼ cup flour
- 2 cups granulated sugar

DIRECTIONS

FOR THE CRUST:

1. Preheat oven to 350 degrees.
2. Mix together butter, powdered sugar, and flour until dough forms.
3. Press into a greased 9 by 13-inch glass baking dish.
4. Bake 20-25 minutes.
5. Cool for 10 minutes.

FOR THE FILLING:

1. Beat eggs; mix in remaining ingredients.
2. Pour over crust.
3. Bake 20–25 minutes until the center of the filling is cooked through.
4. Cool for 30 minutes; sprinkle powdered sugar on top before serving.

I store my lemon bars in the refrigerator because I like eating them very cold.

JARYN'S SCONES, TWO WAYS:
LEMON BLUEBERRY & ORANGE CRANBERRY

INGREDIENTS

- 4 cups all-purpose flour
- 2 tablespoons baking powder
- 1½ teaspoons kosher salt
- ⅔ cup sugar
- I cup butter, chopped into small pieces and very cold
- I cup heavy cream, plus a little extra for brushing on top
- 2 eggs

MIX-INS FOR LEMON BLUEBERRY SCONES:

- zest of one lemon
- I cup blueberries

MIX-INS FOR ORANGE CRANBERRY SCONES:

- zest of one orange
- I cup dried cranberries

FOR THE GLAZE:

- 2 cups powdered sugar, divided
- 2 tablespoons lemon juice
- 2 tablespoons orange juice
- ½ teaspoon almond extract

DIRECTIONS

1. Preheat oven to 400 degrees. Prepare two baking sheets with parchment paper.
2. In the bowl of an electric mixer, mix together flour, baking powder, salt, and sugar.
3. Add butter and mix on low until the butter is the size of small peas.
4. In a separate bowl, whisk together heavy cream and eggs; add to flour mixture and beat on low until just combined.
5. Dump roughly half of the dough onto the counter.
6. In that half, add lemon zest and quickly knead the dough until zest is incorporated, making sure the dough remains cold and the butter does not begin to melt.
7. Shape into a round disk, about ¾ inch thick.
8. Press blueberries into the top of the dough, and cut like a pizza into 8 triangles.
9. Transfer triangles onto a parchment-lined baking sheet.
10. Leave the other half of the dough in the bowl of the mixer.

DIRECTIONS CONT.

11. Add orange zest and dried cranberries.
12. Quickly mix until just combined.
13. Dump onto counter and shape into a round disk, about ¾ inch thick, making sure the dough remains cold.
14. Cut like the other dough, into 8 triangles.
15. Transfer to the other parchment-lined baking sheet.
16. Brush all scone tops with heavy cream, and bake for 18–20 minutes.
17. When the scones are ready, they will be brown on top and firm to the touch.
18. Remove and let cool for about 10 minutes before drizzling the glaze on top.
19. Top with Devonshire or clotted cream and enjoy every crumb at your next tea party!

FOR THE LEMON GLAZE

1. Swiftly mix together with a fork 1 cup powdered sugar and 2 tablespoons lemon juice.
2. Drizzle on blueberry scones.

FOR THE ORANGE GLAZE

1. Mix together in the same fashion the remaining 1 cup powdered sugar, 2 tablespoons orange juice, and ½ teaspoon almond extract.
2. Drizzle on cranberry scones.

recipe six

THE PERFECT CUP OF TEA

DIRECTIONS

1. Bring fresh water to a boil.
2. Measure 1 teaspoon loose leaf tea into a mesh tea ball infuser or empty tea bag for every 8-ounce cup of hot water; place infuser in your favorite porcelain teacup.
3. Pour water directly on leaves.
4. Let steep.
5. Add milk, honey, or lemon to your liking.

STEEPING LENGTH

GREEN TEA

2–3 minutes

OOLONG TEA

3–4 minutes

BLACK TEA

4–5 minutes

HERBAL TEA

5–7 minutes

HERE ARE A FEW OTHER FAVORITE THINGS WE DO IN MAY

BERRY PICKING
Find a local U-pick strawberry or blueberry farm and let the juices drip down your face as you taste your pickings. Use the blueberries in the scone recipe found in this chapter.

RUN A 5K
Get your neighbors together early Memorial Day morning for a 5k run. As you run or walk, remember the individuals who have sacrificed their lives for our country.

CELEBRATE CINCO DE MAYO
Celebrate Cinco de Mayo with chips, salsa, guacamole, horchata, tacos, and amigos.

START A BOOK CLUB
Mine has been going strong for eight years now, and the women in it are some of my closest friends. We meet together every month to catch up, eat, laugh, cry, and talk about good books.

REFRESH AND REJUVENATE
Take some time away to refresh and rejuvenate your well-being as a woman—whether it be doing yoga, getting a pedicure, reading a good book alone at the beach, or getting a massage. You'll return home with a sense of peace and confidence that you can conquer anything (even if it is just that giant pile of laundry that has been waiting to be folded for days).

extra traditions

june

june

One thing is for sure, though: we must kick off summer with our Solstice Kick-Off Extravaganza.

SOLSTICE KICK-OFF
EXTRAVAGANZA

SOLSTICE KICK-OFF EXTRAVAGANZA

june's

The sun is hot and vibrant, school is out, and schedules are beginning to ebb—the longest day of the year is definitely a reason to celebrate.

Before school gets out, I ask the kids to make lists of activities they would like to do during the summer. Then we combine them all and narrow our family summer bucket list down to about twenty items and transcribe them onto a long scroll of butcher paper to hang in our kitchen.

The funny thing is that there isn't much of a change in our list from year to year. A few years back, we went to the pet store and bought frilly beta fish, so now the kids hope to get new fish every summer. Another must-do item on the list is to play with cousins. The kids can never get enough of their cousins, and with busy schedules during the school year, we end up seeing them only about once a month. But in the summer, we practically live with them. The beach is also a must, along with the county fair.

One thing is for sure, though: we must kick off summer with our Solstice Kick-Off Extravaganza.

For this event, we go by the phrase, "The more the merrier." We send an online invitation out to many friends from our community in hopes that they will join us in celebrating the longest day of the year. Making it really easy, we ask friends to bring side dishes or desserts to share, and Dylan grills up hotdogs and brats at our local park. We make sure to have baskets of sunflower seeds, Cracker Jacks, and Big League Chew for everyone to snack on during a game of kickball, because what's a ballgame without Big League Chew?

I love a good kickball competition. I love that kids and adults alike get their game on. I love seeing Ryan Bush pushing his kids aside as they're running the bases. And I love seeing the winning team gloat. (As long as I'm on that winning team.)

We spend the warm evening catching up with beloved friends, eating our all-American ballfield dinners, and kicking the ball as hard as we can. Gia and I hold hands as we run the bases together after kicking the ball with all of our might. This is the kind of fun that I want our children to remember forever. And what a way to kick off summer!

COWBOY CAVIAR

Cowboy Caviar is a simple appetizer for a laid-back event such as our Solstice Kick-Off. Pair it with tortilla chips, and you'll have yourself an addicting setup that will attract a crowd.

INGREDIENTS

- 15-ounce can black beans, drained and rinsed
- 2 cups fresh corn, cut off the cob
- 2 roma tomatoes, diced
- 2 avocados, diced
- ¼ cup red onion, minced
- 1 small jalapeño, seeds removed and diced very small (only if you like it hot)
- fresh cilantro as a garnish

DRESSING

- 2 tablespoons red wine vinegar
- 2 tablespoons lime juice
- 1 teaspoon granulated sugar or honey
- 1 clove garlic
- ⅓ cup olive oil
- ½ teaspoon salt
- cracked pepper to taste

DIRECTIONS

FOR THE COWBOY CAVIAR:

1. Combine above ingredients in a medium bowl.
2. Toss with dressing.
3. Serve with tortilla chips.

FOR THE DRESSING:

1. Combine dressing ingredients in a jar fitted with a lid.
2. Shake well.

You may have excess dressing to save for another salad, depending on how much dressing you like.

recipe two

ANGIE'S S'MORE COOKIE BARS

These s'more bars scream of summertime and bonfires, even if there isn't a
bonfire in sight. They feed a large crowd, so they are a perfect dessert to share
at our Solstice Kick-Off Extravaganza.

INGREDIENTS

CRUST:

- 28 full graham crackers
- 1 cup butter, melted

COOKIE TOPPING:

- 1 cup butter, room
  temperature
- 1½ cups granulated sugar
- 1 cup brown sugar
- 2 large eggs
- 1 teaspoon vanilla extract
- 2½ cups all-purpose flour
- 1 teaspoon baking soda
- 1 teaspoon salt
- 2 cups semisweet chocolate
  chips
- 1 cup mini marshmallows,
  plus some extra for the top
- 2 Hershey's milk chocolate
  bars, broken

DIRECTIONS

FOR THE CRUST:

1. In a food processor, combine graham
   crackers and melted butter.
2. Press into a 10 by 13-inch bar pan lined
   with parchment paper.

FOR THE COOKIE TOPPING:

1. Preheat oven to 350 degrees.
2. Cream together butter and sugars.
3. Mix in eggs and vanilla.
4. In a separate bowl, combine flour,
   baking soda, and salt.
5. Slowly mix into butter mixture.
6. Once combined, fold in chocolate chips
   and marshmallows.
7. Spoon cookie dough as evenly as
   possible onto graham cracker crust.
8. Bake for about 20 minutes.
9. Dough will spread as it cooks to fill in
   gaps.
10. While bars are in the oven, break
    chocolate bars into sections and place
    in freezer.
11. About 8–10 minutes before bars are
    finished baking, sprinkle remaining
    marshmallows on top, and then return
    to oven to finish baking.
12. When bars come out of the oven,
    carefully place broken chocolate bar
    pieces on top.
13. Let cool completely before cutting.

extra traditions

HERE ARE A FEW OTHER FAVORITE THINGS WE DO IN JUNE

NATIONAL DOUGHNUT DAY

Celebrate National Doughnut Day on June 1!

FATHER'S DAY INTERVIEWS

On videotape, interview your children each year answering the same questions. Present it to their dad for Father's Day, and watch how they grow over the years.

SUMMER BUCKET LIST

Unroll butcher paper, and write down your summer bucket list with markers. Get the kids involved by adding their ideas, then ask them to illustrate what they want to do.

SUMMER BASKET

On the last day of school, surprise your children with a summer basket. Fill it with squirt guns, snacks, pool toys, swim goggles, sunscreen, and fun drinks to keep them hydrated.

VISIT THE DRIVE-IN

If your town has a drive-in movie theater, fill your car with blankets and pillows and load the family in for a cozy evening.

COUNTY FAIR

Visit the county fair. Need I say more?

june

. . . .

"Live in the
sunshine, swim
the sea, drink the
wild air . . . "

. . . .

RALPH WALDO EMERSON

july

july

The perfect picnic
begins with the
perfect vibe: low-key,
no-fuss fun . . .

THE PERFECT PICNIC

july's PERFECT PICNIC

In the summertime, we have the same routine every Friday. Our day begins as I text multiple families and invite them to enjoy an evening picnic and family-friendly concert at the park with us. Fridays in the summer are a lot of work, but when we are surrounded by friends on hand-tied quilts and swaying to local bands at the end of the day, they are so worth it. When I get the final headcount, the kids and I scramble to the park before ten in the morning to save our spots by laying out every blanket from our house. Especially our favorite Hulk blanket.

Hulk is one of those furry blankets you find clothes-pinned for all to see at a gas station or in Mexico or at the county swap meet. My sister Jenny gave him to us years ago, and he is a well-recognized member of our family. Hulk joins us in all of his muscular green physique to late-night baseball games, midday soccer games, beach parties, and picnics at the park. He's green, black, purple, and brown, so he is versatile and camouflagable, easily hiding the dirt, mud, and food that tramps along with kids.

I have to thank my dear friend Lindsey Tanner for introducing us to these local concerts. When we moved into our area, she and Jake were the first people to invite us out to dinner and to every other church and social activity from then on. Lindsey is a drop-dead gorgeous bombshell with legs as long as the Brooklyn Bridge and Cherokee chiseled cheekbones, all rolled up in a package of

Southern charm. Her laugh is loud and silly, and she has the appetite of two teenage boys. What I love the most about Lindsey is that she makes everyone feel included and loved. And a bonus—she initiates! Lindsey invited us to our first of many Carlsbad summer concerts, and for this I will forever be indebted.

Every Friday, after reserving our prime real estate on the lawn of the baseball field, the kids and I drive home to prepare some items for our picnic.

The perfect picnic begins with the perfect vibe—low-key, no-fuss fun—but you can make it as easy or as complicated as you want it to be. My idea of a perfect picnic includes the ones I love, a giant quilt to fit the entire family on, our table-in-a-bag, great music, and delicious food.

You can be anywhere to enjoy your perfect picnic: a local park, the beach, a calm lake, deep in the woods, the rooftop of your big city apartment building, or even your own backyard. In this case, our family enjoys the picnic at our local summer family-friendly concert.

I have a couple go-to salads that I prepare in advance: Megan's Spinach Tortellini Salad and Jessica's Orzo Salad. I divvy up servings into Chinese takeout boxes for easy disposability at the concert. I'm usually all about going green, but I give myself a night off once in a while, and this is one of those times. My favorite dessert to bake for the concerts at the park is my friend Dee Dee's Buttermilk

Banana Bread with an Orange-Almond Glaze. I lovingly package up slices of this bread with orange slices, ripe peaches, and fresh whipped cream to savor at the end of our evening.

Parking is always a situation at the concerts, so Dylan drops us all off at the curb with our picnic basket stocked with salads, desserts, a baguette, Barefoot Contessa's Tomato Crostini with Whipped Feta, chips, and a little bubbly; our Costco Tommy Bahama beach chairs that every other person at the concert has; and our table-in-a-bag. This used to be even more of an ordeal when we had babies. A car seat, diaper bag, and nursing cover were always in that mix—and can you imagine me lugging it all into the park with little people tugging at my maxi dress? But Dylan has the more difficult job: finding a place to park. Pretty much every space in the city is taken, so he does his best, and he's smart enough to bring a skateboard for the long distances.

Now that I have some older helpers, a.k.a. Seven and Shade, things are much easier. So as Seven screws the table-in-a-bag together, I unload our dinner and remember the time years ago when we came with the Gwilliams. Seven was five and a half and spent the evening dancing with Auden in his arms, dipping her and swaying to the music. They were so cute. Now, eight years later, Seven acts too old to dance, and he plays tag with friends while the rest of us groove away to the reggae music.

Once everything is set up, we finally get the chance to revel in our community, to let loose with the people who also chose this wonderful city as their home. We share food, stories, dancing, and laughter with the friends we cheer at soccer games with, people we worship at church with, and acquaintances we run into at the grocery store.

As Dylan and I steal away quiet moments together before getting interrupted by our little people, I remind myself to thank dear Lindsey for inviting us to these concerts over eight years ago. We joined this community of culture lovers of all ages—kids, adults, and wrinkly grandpas. And through this tradition, I hope our children will develop a sense of culture and community, a quality that I find very important to pass on to future generations.

JESSICA'S ORZO SALAD

INGREDIENTS

- ¼ cup red wine vinegar
- 2 tablespoons fresh lemon juice
- I teaspoon honey
- ½ cup olive oil
- I pound orzo
- 2–3 teaspoons salt
- 2 cups halved grape tomatoes
- 7 ounces crumbled feta cheese
- I cup chopped sweet basil
- I cup chopped green onions
- ½ cup toasted pine nuts

DIRECTIONS

I. Whisk together vinegar, lemon juice, and honey in a small bowl. Gradually whisk in oil. Set aside.

2. Meanwhile, bring water to a boil in a large pot.

3. Add salt to the water.

4. Cook orzo according to package.

5. Strain and let cool.

6. Mix tomatoes, feta, basil, and green onions into cooled orzo.

7. Add vinaigrette and toss to coat.

8. Season with salt and pepper.

9. Let stand at room temperature.

10. Add pine nuts just before serving and toss.

recipe two

DEE DEE'S BUTTERMILK BANANA BREAD WITH AN ORANGE-ALMOND GLAZE

INGREDIENTS

- 3 cups flour

- 1½ teaspoons salt

- 1½ teaspoons baking soda

- 2½ cups granulated sugar

- 3 eggs

- 1 cup buttermilk (or 1 cup milk plus 2 teaspoons white vinegar)

- 1½ teaspoons vanilla

- 1½ teaspoons pure almond extract

- 1 cup canola oil (or olive oil)

- 3 ripe bananas, mashed

FOR THE GLAZE, COMBINE:

- 1 tablespoon melted butter

- ¾ cup granulated sugar

- ¼ cup orange juice

- ½ teaspoon vanilla

- ½ teaspoon almond extract

DIRECTIONS

1. Preheat the oven to 325 degrees.
2. Grease two glass loaf pans.
3. In a large mixing bowl, combine flour, salt, baking soda, and sugar.
4. Add eggs, buttermilk, vanilla, almond extract, oil, and mashed bananas to mixture.
5. Mix together until just combined.
6. Pour batter into 2 greased loaf pans, and bake for about 60-75 minutes, until an inserted toothpick or wooden skewer comes out clean.
7. Remove from oven and poke holes into bread with wooden skewer.
8. Let cool slightly, and remove from pans.
9. Pour glaze over top.
10. Slice up, and enjoy with sliced peaches and fresh whipped cream.

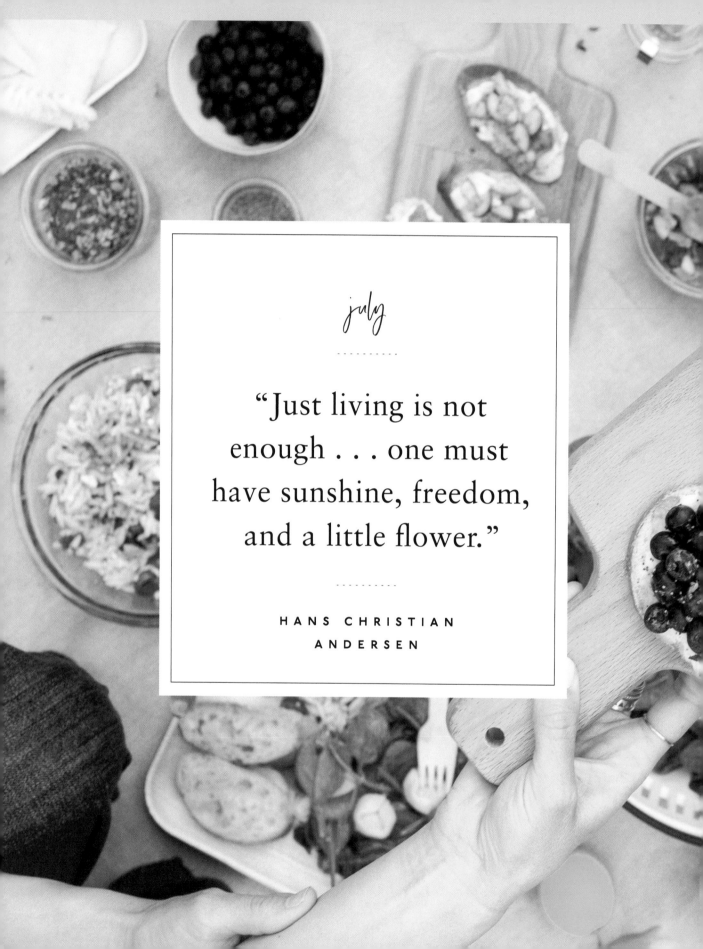

july

"Just living is not enough . . . one must have sunshine, freedom, and a little flower."

HANS CHRISTIAN
ANDERSEN

MEGAN'S SPINACH AND TORTELLINI SALAD

Megan brought this salad along with her heavenly homemade crescent rolls to our family when Baby Melrose was born. This salad is so refreshing, it practically begs to be taken to a concert in the park. For the kids, I'll usually pack the tortellini on its own with a side of mandarin oranges.

INGREDIENTS

SWEET SESAME DRESSING:

- ¾ cup sugar
- ¼ cup red wine vinegar
- ¼ cup olive oil
- ½ teaspoon salt
- ¼ teaspoon paprika
- 1 tablespoon grated onion
- 1 tablespoon toasted sesame seeds

FOR THE SALAD:

- 1 bag baby spinach
- 1 pound tortellini (I buy mine from Trader Joe's because it is the best price)
- 1 pound bacon, cooked and broken up into small pieces (optional)
- 1 pound chicken breasts, cooked and shredded (optional)
- 2 15-ounce cans mandarin oranges, drained
- 1 avocado
- ½ cup slivered almonds
- ½ cup dried cranberries

DIRECTIONS

FOR THE DRESSING:

1. Bring sugar and vinegar to a boil in a small saucepan.
2. Remove from heat when sugar has dissolved; add remaining ingredients.

Dressing can be made a day or two in advance and placed in refrigerator.

FOR THE SALAD:

1. Layer all ingredients on top of the spinach.
2. Drizzle with sweet sesame dressing; toss and serve.

HERE ARE A FEW OTHER FAVORITE THINGS WE DO IN JULY

BE THOUGHTFUL THURSDAYS

While the kids are out of school, participate in "Be Thoughtful Thursdays." Every Thursday, take bunches of balloons to the park and share them with other kids. Pass out flowers to ladies exiting the grocery store. Bake cookies for your neighbor. The possibilities are endless!

FOURTH OF JULY CELEBRATION

Make Martha Stewart's Flag Cake for your Fourth of July celebration.

FAMILY TRIP

Include your children in helping you plan a family trip. Depending on their ages, ask your children to make packing lists, help with the vacation budget and booking hotels, or plan meals.

ADVENTURE BACKPACKS

Pack adventure backpacks and explore a new beach, a new park, or a hiking trail you have never been on. Include snacks, water bottles, bandages, binoculars, a nature journal, and colored pencils in the pack.

HOMEMADE ICE CREAM

Get the ice cream maker out and churn some good old-fashioned vanilla ice cream.

BASTILLE DAY

Turn your "perfect picnic" into a gussied-up picnic with Parisian croissants, baguettes, cheeses, quiche, and macarons in celebration of Bastille Day on July 14.

august

august

The evening before school begins is filled with elegant food, goals for the school year, and everlasting memories.

SCHOOL YEAR'S EVE

august's # SCHOOL YEAR'S EVE

This evening our table is adorned with pressed white linens, my great-great grandmother's fine china painted with delicate periwinkle and rose-colored flowers, my mother-in-law's silver goblets filled with sparkling drinks, and flickering candles casting magnificent glows on the kitchen walls.

The evening before school begins is filled with elegant food, goals for the school year, and everlasting memories. I read about this tradition on Stephanie Nielson's blog, *Nie Nie Dialogues*, several years ago and adored everything about it. I fell in love with her emphasis on a theme for the new school year and fell more in love with how special she made her children feel. Every year, I can hardly wait to view her blog, gushing over all of the gorgeous photographs filled with details, crowns, glitter, flowers, party dresses, bowties, and love.

We call it our School Year's Eve Dinner, and for this particular school year, we are focusing on the theme "You are going to soar!" We hope that our children will spread their wings of confidence and will truly soar regardless of the challenges they might face.

After studying *The Conscious Parent* by Shefali Tsabary, Dylan and I were moved to share with our children that we were not as concerned with the grades they got in school as we were in their process of learning. We want our children to love to learn. To have a curiosity in life and about other people. To invest themselves in reveling in other cultures. With these passions, they will soar.

If you are looking for some ideas of themes for your next School Year's Eve dinner, you will find some of our family's past themes below. I also urge you to head over to Stephanie Nielson's blog and find undeniable inspiration there.

OUR FAMILY'S PAST THEMES

RESPECT ALL

One of our young boys (I'm not going to name names) needed a lesson on being respectful this particular year. I remember him yelling at me one day, "You're mean, Mom!" My heart was crushed. I was depleted and deflated in that moment. But now, as a seasoned mom, I

> **We hope that our children will spread their wings of confidence and regardless of the challenges . . . they will truly soar.**

know that those words are completely normal at this age, and I have since then heard the other three yell them at me once or twice (or maybe twenty times?). But since I was a first-time mom, I took it to heart.

I hoped my son would not be the disrespectful Wild Thing for his new preschool teacher. I introduced our new tradition of a School Year's Eve Dinner with a theme for the school year. We blasted Aretha Franklin's "Respect" while dancing around the kitchen. I made Seven's favorite fancy dinner and our young family made a vow to respect all.

BE A HERO

As parents of two young boys who lived and breathed Legos, trains, dirt, and superheroes, Dylan and I incorporated their love into our theme for this particular preschool year. I made red felt superhero capes with "Super Seven" and "Super Shade" written on the backs in black felt

block letters. To us, being a hero meant opening our eyes, always looking for people to save. To help, to open doors for, to include, to comfort.

This was the year I began to teach our boys how to be young gentlemen. For me,

one of the most important qualities a young man should have is a polite manner to other human beings. If a woman drops her wallet on the floor, I hope my boys will be the first to pick it up for her. If a lady is carrying bags of heavy groceries to her car, I urge my boys to help her with her bags. When we are going through a doorway, I stop and stand

use for rest time. Some kids even fall asleep in class at the beginning of the year. At our School Year's Eve Dinner, I tied a turquoise towel with Seven's name in red embroidered letters around his chair at the dinner table.

Seven is our firstborn. As a young boy, when he didn't get things right the first time, he would get so frustrated with himself that he would want to give up. For this school year, we wanted to instill in him the phrase "practice, practice, pratice." He doesn't have to get it right the first time. Or the second. Or the third. Just the art of practicing and never giving up is what is important. This was also the year Shade started preschool, and we wanted him to know the same thing: never giving up is what is important, not perfection.

there until one of my sons opens the door for me. This quality shows awareness of others instead of self. It is commendable and service-oriented. And maybe this quality will be what the girls love about my boys when they are looking to get married.

PRACTICE, PRACTICE, PRACTICE

Seven was ready for his first year of kindergarten, and I couldn't hold the tears back as we dropped him off on his first day. He had a brand-new backpack, brand-new outfit, and brand-new sense of being a big kid. Since our school district holds full-day kindergarten, the teachers ask that the children have a blanket or towel that they can

NEVER GIVE UP

Seven began the new school year with a challenge at hand. He had finally gotten into our dual-language immersion program after remaining on the wait-list his entire year of kindergarten. For his first-grade school year, he would be the only student in his class who did not have a year of Spanish under his belt.

Feeling anxious, nervous, and excited, he lived by our motto, "Never give up." At the beginning of the school year, I imagined Seven sitting cross-legged with a glazed-over stare, completely clueless as to what was going on in the classroom with the teacher not speaking a lick of English. I imagined him trying to communicate and giving up. I would cry for him while he was at school, but every day Seven returned home with a smile on his face, ready to work with me an extra hour and a half on Spanish vocabulary, reading in Spanish, and math written only in Spanish. I needed to cut it out and pull myself together! I learned something about my son this year. He was determined, and he never gave up.

GO FOR IT

With Seven in second grade and Shade now entering kindergarten, Shade was grandfathered into the dual-language immersion program. I aimed to make it a more positive experience for myself this year by sending them off with the theme "Go For It."

Shade was ready and determined to learn, and I was not going to sit at home crying and worrying about him all day long. First of all, he had the most amazing and capable teacher, who we grew to see as another member of our family. Second of all, Shade was happy and had a positive attitude. And third, what good does it do to sit around worrying? This school year was amazing in so many ways for both Seven and Shade. They really went for it.

BE A LIGHT

For this particular school year, Dylan and I talked to the kids about what being a light means to us. It is standing up for what you believe in, no matter what. It means choosing what is right when others aren't. It means being an example to others, being the kind of kid who other people want to hang around because they look for ways to help everyone feel included.

When Dylan and I presented this theme, we handed each of the kids a pure white taper candle. I lit one and held it to the wick of Seven's candle. Seven held his to the wick of Shade's, then Shade shared his light with Melrose, and Melrose to Gia. In the end, Gia shared her flame with Dylan. We talked about how light and warmth and happiness can spread to others. We encouraged the kids to look for ways to share their light. Every day that school year, I sent the kids out the door reminding them to "be a light."

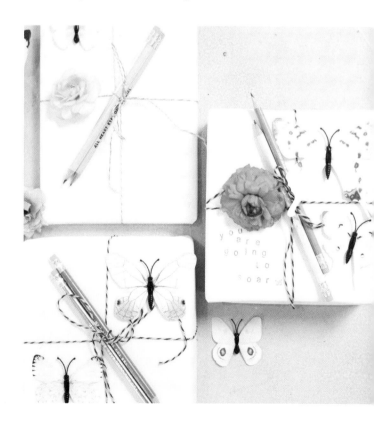

BECAUSE I HAVE BEEN GIVEN MUCH, I TOO MUST GIVE

My mind was drawing a blank one year, and I couldn't come up with a theme to save my life. I wanted it to be perfect. I asked Dylan if he had any ideas, and he immediately came up with, "Because I have been given much, I too must give." These are words to a well-known hymn at our church, and they would become our new motto for the school year.

As a family, we committed to volunteer more in our community and school. We committed to give more, serve more, and look for creative ways to help others. We weren't just focusing on money and material things either but, more importantly, our time, kind words of encouragement, positive thoughts, and prayers.

We had a magical evening that night as a family sitting around our fire table, enjoying our Italian sodas and a delicious meal in our courtyard. With full bellies, we all leaned back to listen as Seven and Dylan plucked at their guitars—our courtyard echoing with the hum of peace and contentment. I find such joy in these moments. I didn't want the night to end, but the kids needed rest for their big day. We washed up, Dylan poured blessings upon our children, and we lit our candles; symbolizing all the light we have to give to others. It was a good night.

GRANDMA MARYANNE'S GARLIC BREAD

INGREDIENTS

- 1 loaf of French bread
- 8 tablespoons butter
- 4 garlic cloves, minced (I use the frozen crushed garlic cubes from Trader Joe's)
- ½ cup parmesan cheese, plus more for top
- 2 teaspoons dried parsley

DIRECTIONS

1. Cut bread lengthwise down the center to make two long pieces.
2. Set aside on a baking sheet lined with tinfoil.
3. Melt butter in a small saucepan.
4. Add garlic and ½ cup parmesan cheese.
5. Stir well, remove from heat, and carefully pour evenly onto both halves of the French bread.
6. Sprinkle with more parmesan cheese and dried parsley flakes.
7. Broil in oven at a high broil until golden brown.
8. Remove from oven and slice into pieces.

recipe two

ITALIAN SODAS

Italian sodas are our thing. Dylan is the master mixologist when we invite friends into our home for dinner. When I think back to all of the major parties, baby showers, or dinners we have had, Italian sodas are always in attendance.

In preparation, I place on our counter various Torani syrups—raspberry, vanilla, coconut, passion fruit, strawberry, peach—along with sparkling water, ice, heavy whipping cream, whipped cream, cups, lids, and straws. Then Dylan works his magic. He takes orders, marks up guests' cups with their names, and even asks them to taste-test, making sure their orders are just right, maybe adding a little extra cream here and there. We don't hold back.

INGREDIENTS

MAKES 1 SODA

- 3 tablespoons Torani syrup (my favorite is raspberry)
- 1 cup ice, preferably crushed
- 1 cup sparkling water
- 1 tablespoon heavy cream
- whipped cream

DIRECTIONS

1. In a glass or goblet, pour Torani syrup (mixing flavors is fun).
2. Add ice, then sparkling water.
3. Pour in cream, and mix well with a straw.
4. Top with whipped cream.

august

"You're off to great places. Today is your day! Your mountain is waiting, so . . . get on your way!"

DR. SEUSS

recipe three

JARYN'S FAVORITE CHOCOLATE CHIP COOKIES

Chewy chocolate chip cookies with a crisp exterior and soft interior are by far my favorite sweet indulgence. When friends bite into these morsels, they can't quite put their finger on why they taste so good—but they know something is different. My little secret is that I roll the balls of dough in sugar before I bake them, giving them a thin layer of crunchy sweetness.

When we have guests for dinner, I oftentimes make pizookies for dessert, which to me are heaven. I press this cookie dough into ramekins and bake a little longer than the baking time for the cookies. When they come out of the oven—hot, steaming, and gooey—I scoop a mound of creamy vanilla ice cream on top. As the ice cream hits the hot pizookie, pools of cream form, making this dessert one that you will want to just dive into. Utterly sinful, I tell ya.

INGREDIENTS

- ¾ cup granulated sugar, plus extra for rolling
- ¾ cup packed light brown sugar
- 1 cup butter at room temperature
- 1 teaspoon vanilla extract
- 1 large egg
- 2½ cups all-purpose flour
- 1 teaspoon baking soda
- ½ teaspoon kosher salt
- 2 cups semisweet chocolate chips (did you know See's Candies sells some really good ones?)

DIRECTIONS

1. Heat oven to 350 degrees.
2. Combine sugars and butter with an electric mixer until creamy.
3. Add vanilla and egg; beat well.
4. Add flour, baking soda, and salt.
5. Mix well until a dough forms.
6. Add chocolate chips, and slowly combine.
7. Roll rounded tablespoonfuls of dough into balls and roll in sugar.
8. Drop about two inches apart on baking sheets lined with silpats.
9. Bake 10–12 minutes, and cool on cookie racks.

DIRECTIONS FOR PIZOOKIES

1. Press cookie dough about 1-inch thick into ramekins.
2. Bake about 12–15 minutes.

You'll get a good feel for how long to bake your pizookies depending on how gooey or how well-cooked you like eating them. Dylan likes his underbaked, and I like mine cooked a bit more.

Also, I am not going to give you a number of how many ramekins or what size of ramekins to use, because the possibilities are endless! Sometimes I will bake one small pizookie for just myself, and other times, we will fill up 12 ramekins for a crowd. Another idea is to press the dough into cupcake liners inside muffin tins for young children.

The most important thing to remember is the vanilla ice cream! (And maybe some whipped cream and sprinkles too.)

recipe *four*

JARYN'S PASTA THE AMALFI WAY

INGREDIENTS

- I package angel hair pasta
  (bowties work well too)
- 2 pints heavy cream
- 2 cups grated parmesan cheese
- juice and zest of 2 lemons
- 4 tablespoons sour cream
- salt and pepper to taste
- garnish with chopped chives
  or parsley and lemon slices

DIRECTIONS

1. Cook pasta al dente according to
   package.
2. Meanwhile, in a large saucepan,
   combine cream and parmesan cheese
   until the cheese is melted and the
   cream is at a low simmer.
3. Add lemon zest and juice.
4. Return to a simmer; remove from heat.
5. Mix in sour cream.
6. Set aside.
7. When pasta is finished cooking, drain
   and toss with olive oil in a large pasta
   dish.
8. Pour cream sauce over pasta and top
   with garnishes.

*The sauce soaks into the pasta quickly,
so I like to set aside some of the cream
sauce in a gravy boat to drizzle more on
top as needed.*

recipe five

PAMELA'S ANTIPASTO SALAD

My mom is a salad-making genius. For any event or gathering, we always ask Mom to bring a salad. She hand-tears her lettuce into tiny pieces, and all of her dressings are homemade. Each flavor and ingredient she uses has been carefully chosen to complement the entire meal. I am sharing with you one of her salads that will undeniably make your mouth water. For finicky eaters, separate ingredients into individual bowls and make it a build-your-own salad bar.

INGREDIENTS

FOR THE SALAD:

- I head red leaf lettuce, rinsed, dried and torn into pieces
- 1–2 hearts of romaine, dried, and torn or chopped into pieces
- ½ jar of fire-roasted red peppers, chopped
- ½ jar pepperoncini
- I can garbanzo beans, drained and rinsed
- ½ jar roasted artichokes, drained
- ½ jar hearts of palm, drained and sliced
- mozzarella, freshly grated
- salami, chopped
- tomatoes, chopped
- red onion, sliced very thin

FOR THE DRESSING:

- ¼ cup red wine vinegar
- ¼ cup water
- ¾ cup canola or olive oil
- I clove garlic
- I teaspoon salt
- I teaspoon sugar or honey
- cracked pepper to taste

DIRECTIONS

FOR THE SALAD:

I. Layer salad ingredients into a large bowl and chill in refrigerator until ready to serve.

My mom prefers metal salad bowls because they keep the salads nice and crisp.

FOR THE DRESSING:

I. Add dressing ingredients into a jar with a lid and shake vigorously to combine.

extra traditions

HERE ARE A FEW OTHER FAVORITE THINGS WE DO IN AUGUST

COOKING CLASS

While your children are still out of school for the summer, invite their friends over for a themed cooking class. To keep it manageable, limit your class to about eight kids.

INTERNATIONAL FRIENDS DAY

Drop off a fun surprise to your closest friends on International Friends Day.

FERRAGOSTO CELEBRATION

Make an Italian feast in celebration of Ferragosto. While this holiday has the religious connotation of the ascension of the Virgin Mary into heaven, Italians use it to culminate the summer season by getting their last travels in. If you'd like to go as far as the Italians do, close up shop, disconnect from work, and have one last summer adventure!

WATER WAR

Get out the Slip 'N Slide, water balloons, and squirt guns, and have a water war with friends and neighbors.

STARGAZING

Take advantage of the warm summer nights by staying up late and stargazing. Bring some fun snacks.

september

september

· · · · · · · · · · ·

Their lives have not had to
be grandiose to impact me;
just the comfort of knowing
they were always there and
that I was loved is what
really mattered.

· · · · · · · · · · ·

GRANDPARENT'S DAY

september's GRANDPARENT'S DAY

Both of my grandfathers passed away when I was a young girl, so I don't have many clear memories about them and cling to the ones I do have.

Grandpa Al was Québécois, and his given last name was Hebert (pronounced so beautifully in French, and not so beautifully in English). When he was only five years old, both of his parents passed away during the flu epidemic. His aunt and uncle raised him, and he took on their last name for the rest of his life: Jannard (also pronounced more beautifully in French than English, but isn't everything more beautiful in French?). The one memory that I have of Grandpa Al was of sitting on his lap as a six-year-old and feeling loved. He smelled of cigars and bar soap.

I wasn't too fond of my last name, Jannard, growing up. Telemarketers and substitute teachers would continually mispronounce it, and it always sounded so harsh. But now that I am older and have taken on a new last name, I have come to appreciate the rich history behind my maiden name and the legacy that my father has made with it.

Just last year, Dylan and I took a two-week trip together to celebrate our 15-year anniversary. We began in Chicago with good food, a ball game, and *Hamilton*. We made our way to Niagara Falls; Stowe, Vermont; Montreal; Quebec City; and, finally, Acadia National Park in Maine. We pursued the changing leaves with colors so brilliant that I gasped in awe at every turn.

My favorite stops during that trip were Montreal and Quebec City, not only for the strong French influence that twinkles over those cities and charming Petit Champlain—which is dotted with pumpkins, scarecrows, and hay bales—but also for the tender connections that I felt to my ancestors. They walked on those cobblestone roads that I walked on, they pressed their hands against walls that I pressed my hands against, and they shed tears for their loved ones just as I would do just two months later. I felt at home.

My mother's father, Grandpa Joe, was full Italian with artistry flowing through his veins. When he was visiting our house during St. Patrick's Day one year, he made us all green pancakes before school. He bought me my first pretend makeup set at an indoor swap

meet when I was a little girl. He drew pictures for me to cherish.

For our five-year anniversary, Dylan and I packed our bags and traveled to Italy together, dining on pizza and gelato every single day. Dylan had never been before, so we explored ancient Rome with all of its history, the Amalfi Coast with its beloved Island of Capri, and Sicily with its wondrous catacombs. Dylan's grandma is full Italian, and she and my Grandpa Joe have origins in Prizzi, Sicily.

One day, Dylan and I tracked down a private records office in search of information on our heritage. I felt a connection to something greater that day, and it was pulling the universes of past and present together. It was magnificent.

My dad's mother, Grandma Mary, lived to be 93. She exuded happiness, spunk, and the utmost pride in her children, grandchildren, and great-grandchildren. Her mother passed away in the same flu epidemic that my grandfather's parents passed away in when my grandma was also only five years old. As a young girl, I visited Grandma in Leisure World, the housing community she lived in. We sat on her back porch together pouring water into tiny plastic cups from a pitcher— my first "tea party." We poured all afternoon, and nothing occupied my time that day other than just being in the company of my grandma.

Grandma wore chunky, gaudy clip-on

earrings that tugged at her earlobes. Wafts of her signature perfume trailed behind her, and just recently my friend Erin gifted me a bottle of Tocca's Cleopatra perfume, which threw me back into the arms of my grandma when I sprayed it on. I used to press my firm thumb onto her supple thumb, amazed that her skin didn't bounce back immediately. My imprint rested there awhile. And her imprint now rests with me.

If you could find an angel on earth, it would be Nana. She is the most loving, giving, and positive 89-year-old you will ever meet. She spends two hours every morning praying for other people.

> *All of these small gestures and little details of my grandparents' lives have influenced who I am today.*

She feels for others' pains so deeply and wants the best for everyone.

When my mom was 13 years old, Nana was shot in her leg five times by an ex-boyfriend. He showed up to her workplace and coaxed her outside for a minute to have a chat. After he coldheartedly shot her, he used the last bullet on himself. Nana was in the hospital for a year and a half, while my mom and Uncle Gary lived with Nana's parents during the recovery. Nana is still in a lot of pain, but you would never know it by the unwavering smile on her beautiful face.

Nana gave me pineapple upside-down kisses when I was a little girl, and she has been there for me always. She is at every family event and vacation, and she's witty, fun to talk to, and loved by all the children.

My friends call her Nana, and anyone I introduce her to tells me I have the most beautiful grandma they have ever seen. I wholeheartedly agree. She is beautiful inside and out.

All of these small gestures and little details of my grandparents' lives have influenced who I am today. Their lives have not had to be grandiose to impact me; just the comfort of knowing they were always there and that I was loved is what really mattered.

For Grandparent's Day, we celebrate our grandparents and all of the sacrifices they have made for us.

Seven, Shade, Melrose, and Gia invite their grandparents over for a special dinner and take the reins of the kitchen, excitedly welcoming Grandma Pamela, PopPop, Grandpa Danny, Grandma Nanette, and Nana into our courtyard for a relaxing Sunday afternoon. They act as professional little waiters, taking orders with pads of paper and pencils from behind their ears.

The kids escort the grandparents to their seats around the fire table, leaving them with our favorite El Nopalito chips and salsa, mingling in between dips.

Melrose and Gia play the part by wearing fancy dresses and passing out menus. On the menu: Navajo Tacos. They are easy and fun, and the grandparents get to order their favorite toppings.

Seven and Shade deliver drinks and take orders, then head back into the kitchen to doctor up the tacos, layering chili, lettuce, cheese, tomatoes, avocados, and sour cream atop fried scones. They make their deliveries and keep drinks refilled, asking if there is anything else they can get for their customers.

It is one of those mellow nights with no

expectations. The grandparents are content to just be there. They get to enjoy the company of each other and their grandchildren and let loose a little.

When we lived in Utah, our children didn't get to see their grandparents as often as they would've liked. Thankfully, now that we live back in California where our parents live, we get to see them much more often.

I know most people are in circumstances where they do not live within driving distance of their parents or grandparents. In this case, you can write and send beautiful cards filled with words of gratitude or send a thoughtfully planned care package for Grandparent's Day. Make it personal by capitalizing on something really unique, like sending a pineapple upside-down cake to the grandma who always gave you pineapple upside-down kisses.

It will make their day, and if your grandparents are anything like ours, they will tell all of their friends about it and share the same story over and over again with everyone they come in contact with that entire month.

NAVAJO TACOS
recipe one

When we lived in Utah, we soon learned that fried scones were a thing. Before then, the only scones I was familiar with were those of the English variety (biscuit-like, like the ones I feature in my May chapter). Fried scones essentially are biscuits, rolled out and fried in hot oil. They are sold in Utah at any county fair and other big events with numerous food vendors to choose from. There is even a fast-food restaurant called The Sconecutter that features scone sandwiches, breakfast sandwiches, Navajo Tacos, and dessert scones.

Use your favorite homemade biscuit recipe (my favorite is JoJo's recipe in *Magnolia Table*), go healthy and make the whole-wheat scones from *100 Days of Real Food* by Lisa Leake, or go really easy and use Pillsbury Grands!

DIRECTIONS FOR FRIED SCONES

1. In a frying pan, heat about ½ inch canola oil over medium heat.
2. Roll biscuits out flat with a rolling pin. In batches, fry the biscuits in oil until golden brown on one side, then flip to cook on the other side. Drain on paper towels.
3. Enjoy with a variety of toppings.

NAVAJO TACO TOPPINGS

Here are some great topping ideas for your Navajo Tacos:
- your favorite chili
- shredded lettuce
- shredded cheese
- diced tomatoes
- chopped green onions
- guacamole or diced avocado
- sour cream
- cilantro
- lime slices

FRIED SWEET SCONES

Here are some fun topping ideas for your sweet scones:
- honey butter
- cinnamon and sugar
- whipped cream
- fresh berries
- Nutella
- Speculoos Cookie Butter
- ice cream
- powdered sugar
- caramel sauce

september

· · · · · · · · · ·

"Grandparents
sort of sprinkle
stardust over
the lives of little
children."

· · · · · · · · · ·

ALEX HALEY

extra traditions

HERE ARE A FEW OTHER FAVORITE THINGS WE DO IN SEPTEMBER

APPLE PICKING

Bite into crisp apples while apple picking at your nearest U-pick orchard. With your bounty, go home and bake an apple pie or apple crisp, go bobbing for apples, or bottle up some homemade apple butter and deliver to friends.

APPLE PRINTS

Slice some of your apples crosswise and stamp into paint to make apple prints. Press onto butcher paper to make decorative wrapping paper. For greeting cards, fold a piece of card stock and stamp the apple on the outside of the card, or stamp onto canvas bags for your next farmer's market visit.

GRAPE STOMPING

Locate the nearest grape vineyard and participate in a good ol' fashioned grape stomp. Channel your inner Lucille Ball as you dance in the grapes.

TEACHER QUESTIONNAIRE

At the beginning of the school year, put together a questionnaire to give to your children's teachers of all of their favorite things (breakfast items, treats, fruits, flowers, snacks, etc.). Have your child deliver little surprises throughout the school year.

AUTUMN LEAVES HUNT

Go on a hunt for the best-looking autumn leaves. Use washi tape and twine to make a festive garland.

october

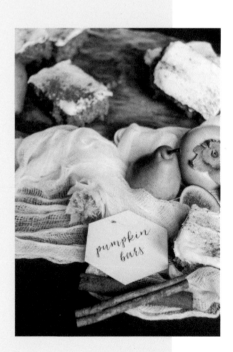

october

- - - - - - - - - -

Bring it on, Fall! Roll me
in your fallen leaves and
spices of cloves, cinnamon,
and nutmeg. Let your cool
breezes dance through my
hair, and send the spooks
haunting my way.

- - - - - - - - - -

FALL FEAST

october's FALL FEAST

Have you ever heard of Julian, the cozy harvest town? Or its famous Julian pies? We are lucky enough to live a little over an hour away from this gold-rush town settled in the Cuyamaca Mountains of California. When we make our annual visit, traversing the curvy roads of the CA-78, we nauseously sing along to cheery tunes, trying to forget how sick this drive always makes us feel. But we still continue to do it every year.

In preparation for our annual Fall Feast, I strap on my denim overalls and pull on my cowboy boots that I've had since high school. It's funny because each year I have this vision of picking apples in the crisp, cool air of the mountains, dressed with scarves and hats and boots. But every year when we visit in September, we are scorched and sweating in the heat of early autumn. These mountains

have not yet cooled, but we refresh by biting into crisp, thirst-quenching apples as we pick—juice dripping down our faces like tiny rivers.

Volcan Valley Apple Farm is our one-stop orchard. It has rows and rows of Fuji, Gala, Empire, Golden Delicious, and Jonathan varieties. Before I shift my car gear into park, the kids are unbuckling and impatiently trying to open the car door, ready to get their feet in the dirt and inhale the fresh air. We purchase buckets to fill with apples and let the kids run free in the orchard, taste-testing as they go. My mom began these field trips with my oldest nephew about 18 years ago. She has since then been bringing her grandchildren to Julian every year for apple-picking season.

Today, Melrose and Gia pluck apples off the trees and polish them on Grandma's flowy, sunflower-printed dress. Lift, twist, pluck. These motions of removing the apples from their trees remind me of an assignment I had in college. For our culminating project in one of my education classes, our teacher Alice Jayne asked us to choose a book and prepare a box filled with activities surrounding the book's theme. Because I love everything fall, I chose a book called *Apples, Apples, Apples*, by Nancy Elizabeth Wallace.

I took this assignment very seriously and spent like a million hours on it, staying up late into the evening working on my box and

> *Little did I know that my future children would pull out this box every fall and enjoy the details that I so carefully put into it.*

spending every extra penny that we had in our newlywed budget on tiny wooden apples from the local craft store. Little did I know that my future children would pull out this box every fall and enjoy the details that I so carefully put into it.

I sit with the kids, slicing apples in half with a sharp knife; pressing the pieces into red, green, and yellow paint; and stamping them onto craft paper, producing gorgeously artful apple prints. Seven and Shade thoughtfully assemble the parts of an apple with the felt pieces I had meticulously cut into tiny shapes of skin, flesh, core, seeds, and stem years ago—my hand aching, becoming a future candidate for carpal tunnel syndrome.

We read *Apples, Apples, Apples* every year before we make the drive out to Julian and are reminded of the proper way to pick an apple—lift, twist, pluck. And gosh, all of the buckets of apples that we drive back home

with, along with our Julian pies and heavenly, moist cider doughnuts, scream for a Fall Feast!

Depending on the year, my stress levels, and our crammed schedules, I modify this event to accommodate our lives.

When Seven turned eight and was baptized into our church, I planned for months a Fall Feast that would feed a hundred. Crunchy Broccoli Waldorf salad, piping hot hand pies filled with every ounce of fall, drippy sharp macaroni and cheese in personal ramekins, cups of creamy pumpkin black bean soup,

chocolate chip cookies rolled in cinnamon and sugar, seasonal pumpkin bars, and apple pear cider were on the menu that year. My mom brought her cheese board with crackers and breads and fig butter. I hauled plump pumpkins and boxy hay bales into our backyard, draping plaid blankets across the coarse straw, lights strung about overhead while friends and family mingled below. Fall will forever be my boyfriend.

After this year's bash, I needed to tone things down a little. I can wear myself out sometimes. I kept it simple by inviting my mom and Nana down for an intimate feast, preparing a lot of the same dishes I had the previous year, but on a much smaller scale— one batch instead of ten batches. I baked

some oat bread, made my favorite tangy pomegranate salad, and simmered pumpkin black bean soup on the stove. The hand pies baked in the oven while pumpkin crème brûlée chilled in the fridge, waiting to be torched and topped with maple leaf cookies.

For our feast this year, I chose to feature our favorite dishes that continue to shine every year. The charcuterie board, pomegranate salad, pumpkin black bean soup, savory sausage and apple hand pies, pumpkin bars, spiced crème brûlée, and apple pie are dishes that urge guests to cozy up and stay late into the evening while welcoming fall. Most of the dishes can be made ahead of time and re-heated before the party starts.

If all of this sounds completely and utterly overwhelming to you, choose one item that you want to flaunt for your feast this year. There is no room for anxiety or guilt while trying to create memories with your family. The only reason I do all of this is that I honestly enjoy being in the kitchen all day cooking for my family. I really do. It brings me the purest of joy providing nourishment for our children. As I work with doughs and yeasts, my soul fills to the brim—just as the yeast proofs, foaming over in a bowl with warm water and sugar. I watch as our children spoon warm soup into their mouths and slather butter all over their bread. And I smile.

recipe one

CHARCUTERIE BOARD

A good cheese board has a strong magnetic force in any gathering. Friends and family members squeeze in tightly to find their places around the board, never wanting to leave. Conversations continue late into the evening, when barriers come down and all are relaxed. Even the tiniest of hands make their way to the table, offering an added sense of joyousness. This amazing board is my mother's, and she drives it 40 minutes down to me whenever I need to borrow it for a gathering. She even fills it with food!

OUR FAVORITE THINGS TO ADD
TO A CHARCUTERIE BOARD

Good news: you can find all of these items at Trader Joe's.

- caramelized onion cheddar
- triple-cream brie
- crumbly gorgonzola
- apple pie cheddar
- honey
- fresh breads
- delicious crackers, including gluten-free
- fresh figs

- candied oranges
- dried apricots
- marcona almonds with rosemary
- candied pecans
- plump grapes
- salami
- apple and fig butters

recipe two

POMEGRANATE SALAD

INGREDIENTS

FOR THE DRESSING:

- ½ cup oil
- 4 tablespoons red wine vinegar
- 4 tablespoons sugar or honey
- 1 teaspoon salt
- ¼ teaspoon cracked pepper
- 3 dashes Tabasco sauce

FOR THE SALAD:

- 2 bunches butter lettuce
- 1 apple, sliced thin
- 1 pear, sliced thin
- 1 avocado, sliced thin
- 1 package pomegranate seeds (or you can fight with a whole pomegranate)
- ¼ cup candied pecans (I heat mine in a pan with sugar until caramelized)
- thin slices of red onion
- blue cheese crumbles

DIRECTIONS

FOR THE DRESSING:

1. Combine all ingredients and quickly whisk until thickened.
2. Refrigerate until ready to use.

FOR THE SALAD:

1. Toss salad with dressing and serve.

pomegranate
salad

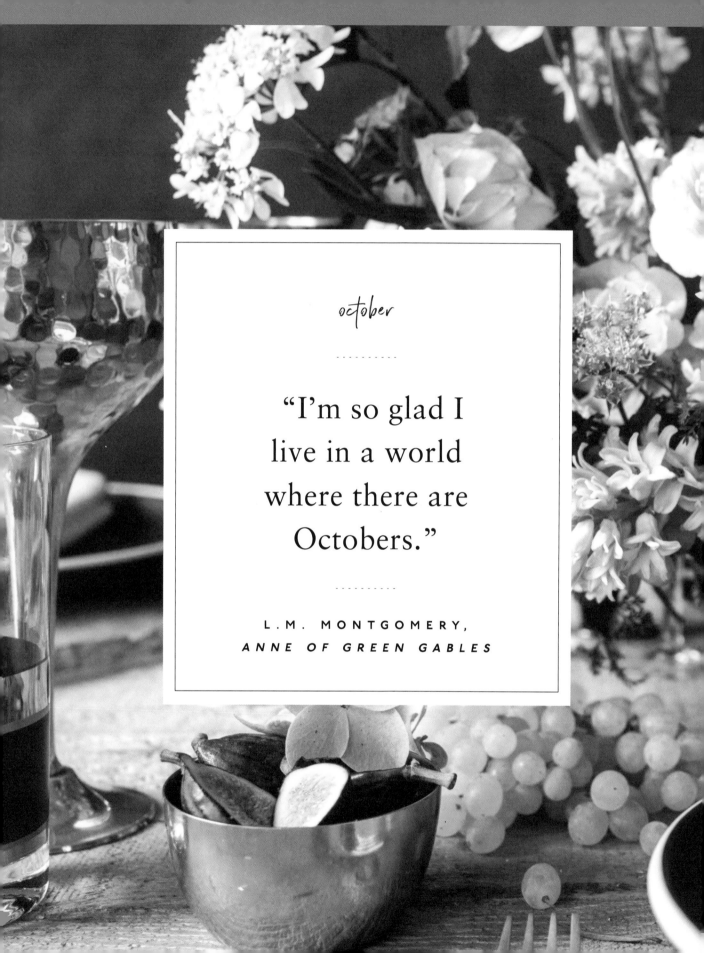

october

. . . .

"I'm so glad I
live in a world
where there are
Octobers."

. . . .

L.M. MONTGOMERY,
ANNE OF GREEN GABLES

pumpkin black
bean soup

WITH SPICY PEPITAS

recipe three

CAROL'S PUMPKIN BLACK BEAN SOUP

My mom walks with her friend Carol every day, and on one of those walks, Carol shared this recipe. We can never get enough of it in the fall!

INGREDIENTS

- 1½ tablespoons olive oil
- 1 onion, diced
- 15-ounce can diced tomatoes
- 15 ounces vegetable broth
- 15-ounce can pumpkin puree
- 15-ounce can black beans, drained and rinsed
- 1 cup cream
- ½ teaspoon curry powder
- ½ teaspoon cumin
- ½ teaspoon chili powder
- salt and pepper to taste

TOPPINGS

- sour cream
- pepitas
- chives
- pomegranate seeds

DIRECTIONS

1. In a large pot, sauté onion in olive oil.
2. Add tomatoes, broth, pumpkin, and black beans.
3. Simmer for 20 minutes.
4. Add cream and spices.
5. Remove from heat and serve with toppings.

SPICED CRÈME BRÛLÉE

INGREDIENTS

- 4 cups heavy cream
- 1 vanilla bean, split and scraped
- ½ cup light brown sugar
- ½ cup sugar
- 8 large egg yolks
- ½ teaspoon ground cinnamon
- ¼ teaspoon ground nutmeg
- 4 teaspoons raw sugar

DIRECTIONS

1. Preheat the oven to 325 degrees.
2. Arrange 8 (½-cup) ramekins in a large metal baking pan.
3. In a medium saucepan, whisk together cream, vanilla bean and its pulp, brown sugar, and sugar.
4. Bring to a simmer over medium-high heat, until sugar is dissolved.
5. Remove from heat and remove vanilla bean.
6. In a medium bowl, whisk egg yolks.
7. Slowly add a little of the cream mixture, whisking briskly.
8. Add the egg mixture to the remaining hot cream; whisk.
9. Add the cinnamon and nutmeg; whisk until smooth.
10. Strain through a fine mesh strainer into a large bowl. Pour evenly into ramekins.
11. Add enough hot water to come halfway up the sides of the ramekins.
12. Bake until just set in the center, 45–55 minutes.
13. Remove from the oven and refrigerate until well chilled, at least 3 hours, or overnight.
14. Sprinkle each custard with ½ teaspoon raw sugar.
15. Use a kitchen torch to caramelize the sugar on top.

recipe five

MAMA'S PUMPKIN BARS

As long as I can remember, my mom has been pulling pans of pumpkin bars out of the oven every fall. They are essential this time of year. After spreading on cream cheese frosting so smoothly and perfectly, she places little mellowcreme pumpkins one by one on each bar. I cannot go a year without making at least three batches, sometimes even four or five.

INGREDIENTS

FOR THE BARS:

- 4 eggs

- 1 ⅔ cups sugar

- 1 cup oil

- 16-ounce can of pumpkin puree

- 2 cups flour

- 2 teaspoons cinnamon

- 1 teaspoon ground ginger

- 1 teaspoon cloves

- 1 teaspoon salt

- 1 teaspoon baking soda

- 2 teaspoons baking powder

FOR THE FROSTING:

- 6 ounces softened cream cheese

- 1 cup butter, softened

- 4 cups powdered sugar

- 2 teaspoons vanilla

DIRECTIONS

FOR THE BARS:

1. Preheat the oven to 350 degrees.
2. Beat eggs, sugar, oil, and pumpkin until fluffy.
3. In a separate bowl, stir together dry ingredients.
4. Add to pumpkin mixture and combine.
5. Pour into an ungreased 10 by 15 inch pan.
6. Bake for 25 minutes.
7. Let cool; slather with frosting.

FOR THE FROSTING:

1. Beat together cream cheese, butter, and powdered sugar until smooth.
2. Add vanilla, and mix until completely incorporated.

HERE ARE A FEW OTHER FAVORITE THINGS WE DO IN THE FALL

FRIENDSGIVING

Host a Friendsgiving and enlist your friends in preparing different dishes found in this chapter. Or better yet, spend the day cooking them all together in your kitchen while listening to a feel-good fall station on Spotify.

FALL FLORALS

Brighten up your home by filling empty pumpkin puree cans left over from the Pumpkin Black Bean Soup recipe with fresh flowers.

MOVIE NIGHT

Snuggle up with someone you love while watching an old favorite TV show or movie. I rewatch *Felicity* every fall because it reminds me of when my husband and I were dating in college. We used to get together with my roommates once a week to catch up on the jaw-dropping love triangle between Felicity, Ben, and Noel.

PUMPKIN PATCH

Enjoy the day with your son, daughter, niece, nephew, grandchild, or friend at a local pumpkin patch and find the perfect pumpkin to scoop out and serve the Pumpkin Black Bean Soup out of for your Fall Feast.

MUMMY DOGS

Twist crescent rolls around hot dogs and bake in the oven to make kid-friendly "mummy dogs" for your Halloween dinner.

november

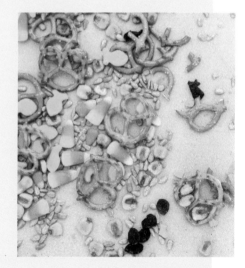

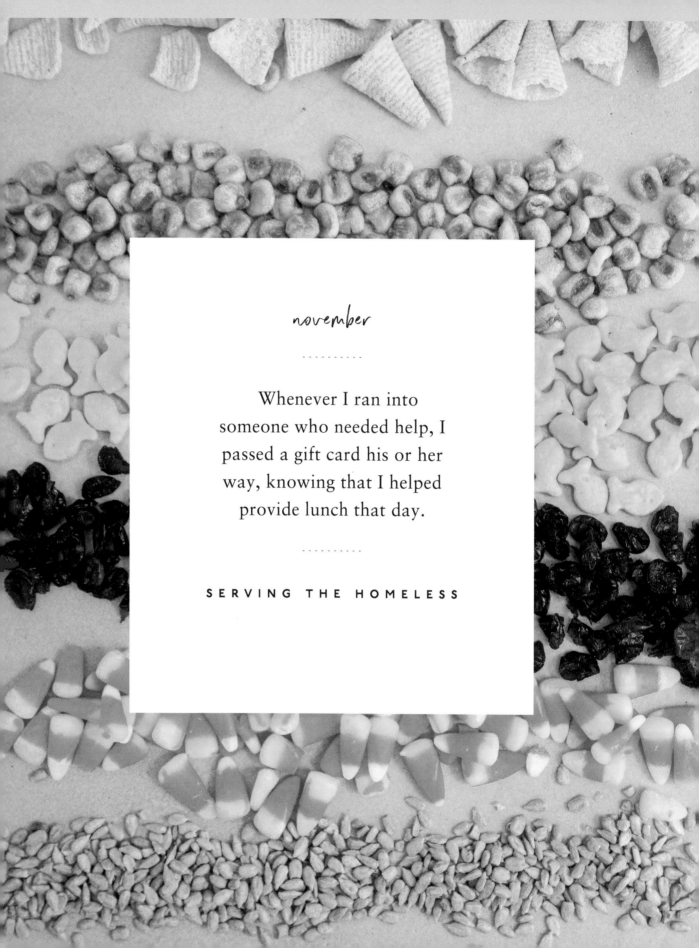

november

· · · · · · · · · ·

Whenever I ran into someone who needed help, I passed a gift card his or her way, knowing that I helped provide lunch that day.

· · · · · · · · · ·

SERVING THE HOMELESS

november's SERVING THE HOMELESS

I have celebrated Thanksgiving in many different locations the last few years: our old house in Utah, Dylan's aunt and uncle's house, a buffet dinner at a grand hotel in a small town in Utah, my mom and stepdad's house, my in-laws' house, Granny and Grandpa's country club, Mexico, and now our home in California. The places have changed, but the feelings have not. Feelings of gratitude, of family togetherness, of hot food, of bursting buttons around the waistline—but, mostly, of a bursting and thankful heart.

My parents are divorced, and as kids, my siblings and I always celebrated Thanksgiving morning with my dad, enjoying a huge breakfast that we all made together: scrambled eggs, crispy bacon, and waffles dripping with syrup and fresh whipped cream. Even though it has been years since I have enjoyed Thanksgiving breakfast with my dad now that I am married with my own children, I have continued this tradition of a delicious breakfast in our own home.

When Seven was tiny and I was pregnant with Shade, my dad took the family (including my siblings and their kids) on a trip to Acapulco. One morning, as we ate gooey huevos rancheros, we belly-laughed over stories of us as kids. I have never seen my dad laugh so hard in his life, tears gushing down his face. Even though this vacation didn't take place in November, the huevos rancheros became a symbol of breakfast with my dad, and I adopted this menu item to serve to my family for Thanksgiving breakfast every year.

Now, as Dylan, the kids, and I fill our bellies each Thanksgiving morning, I reflect on the legacy my dad has passed down to us. I don't think he even knows this.

Even though we have celebrated the Thanksgiving holiday in many different places over the years, we always get together with my in-laws on or as close to Thanksgiving Day as possible. My in-laws, Danny and Nanette, started the tradition of assembling care bags to hand out to those in need during the holiday season.

We all form a traditional assembly line at their kitchen table to make bags for the homeless, dropping granola bars and Slim Jims and fruit snacks and baby wipes and new socks and water bottles from Costco into gallon-size Ziploc bags. Our children write encouraging words like "Have a good day" and "Happy Holidays"—filling them to the brim.

Dylan, the kids, and I ended up with ten bags this year to give away throughout the month of December to anyone who needed a little extra during the Christmas season. The kids loved driving through town looking for people holding their cardboard signs asking for help. Our favorite experience is when we handed a care bag out the window to a man in downtown San Diego one warm, Santa Ana afternoon, and he responded, "Do you have an extra one for my friend?" Thankfully we had one bag left in the car, and out from behind a

I hope that, through these small acts of kindness, our children will learn to have compassion toward others and be able to feel that joy that comes through serving others.

I hope that, through these small acts of kindness, our children will learn to have compassion toward others and be able to feel that joy that comes through serving others. I am grateful to Dylan's parents for providing this conduit in which our children can learn so many life lessons.

street sign peeked his friend, looking hot and thirsty. What a testament of one man looking out for his brother during the holidays.

This small gesture for the homeless reminds me of a project I put together in high school. I researched the reasons people end up homeless (some of them are so tragic and unfair), and I thought of some small ways that I could make a difference in their lives. I purchased five-dollar gift cards from fast food restaurants and kept them in my glove box. Whenever I ran into someone who needed help, I passed a gift card his or her way, knowing that I helped provide lunch that day.

Continuing with this venture, I enlisted a friend to help me make twenty lunches and deliver them in downtown Los Angeles. There was so much gratitude that day. Not only from the people receiving the lunches, but more importantly, in my heart.

november

. . . .

"No one has
ever become poor
from giving."

. . . .

ANNE FRANK

recipe one

PILGRIM BLESSING SNACK

My mom stops by our house with her bag of tricks to make her Pilgrim Blessing Snack with the kids after school in November. They carefully measure pretzels, Bugles, and corn nuts into a big glass jar and crowd around the counter as Grandma reviews the meaning behind each ingredient.

I am grateful to my mom for teaching my children these life lessons of gratitude, and this salty snack stands as a reminder lasting us through the month of November. This lesson of gratitude has such an impact on our kids that every year they ask to bring it to school to share with their classmates.

CORNUCOPIA:

- 2 cups Bugles, representing a bountiful harvest

FOLDED ARMS:

- 2 cups pretzels, representing gratitude and prayer

KERNELS OF CORN:

- 2 cups corn nuts or candy corn, showing that the first winter food was scarce

PLENTIFUL FISH:

- 2 cups goldfish crackers, representing the talents shared by the Native Americans with the Pilgrims

HARVEST OF FRUIT:

- I cup dried cranberries, representing the Thanksgiving tradition

SEEDS:

- I cup sunflower seeds, showing the potential of a bounteous harvest for the next season if well tended

DIRECTIONS:

I. Let children measure out the ingredients and add to a large bowl.
2. Talk about the symbols of each ingredient.
3. Mix well.

HERE ARE A FEW OTHER FAVORITE THINGS WE DO IN NOVEMBER

TURKEY TROT
Join with your community members in running a local Turkey Trot on Thanksgiving morning. Most of them donate the proceeds to local food banks.

PILGRIM BLESSING SNACK
Together with the kids, make the Pilgrim Blessing Snack found in this chapter.

PIE TINS
Make some pie tins filled with surprises and crafts for the hungry kids patiently (or impatiently) waiting to eat Thanksgiving dinner. Inside pie tins, include snacks (maybe even the Pilgrim Blessing Snack), crayons, paper, stickers, stamps, small toys, and Legos. The website One Charming Day has a really cute printable that looks like a pumpkin pie to add to the top of the pie tin.

GRATEFUL PAPER
Hang a long piece of craft paper on the wall of a high-traffic area in your house with some markers nearby. For the entire month, join with the family in adding things that you are grateful for.

HOMEMADE CARDS
Make sweet cards and deliver them to residents of a local nursing home or hospital.

KID'S TABLE

Roll out black chalk paper or black construction paper on the kid's table at Thanksgiving dinner and hand-draw place settings, place markers, and fun phrases like "I am thankful for . . . ," "gobble gobble," and "eat more greens" with a chalk pen.

THANK-YOU NOTES

Write and deliver thank-you notes to the poll volunteers on Election Day.

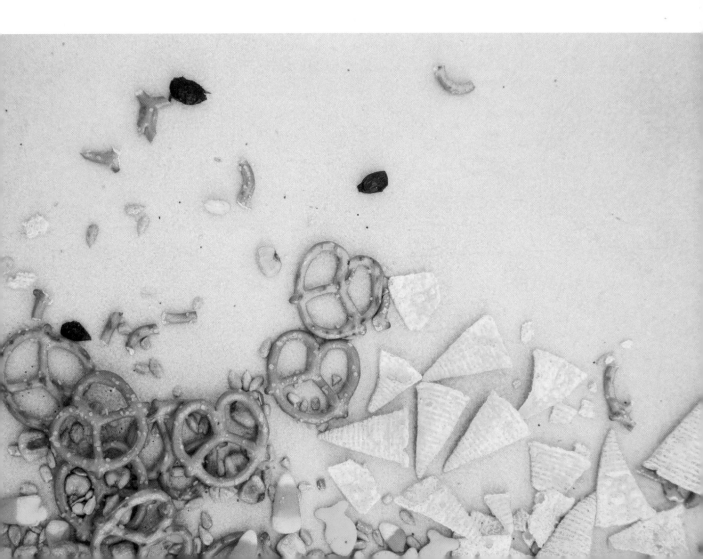

december

december

Welcome to truly the most wonderful time of the year!

SUGAR COOKIE
DECORATING KIT

december's SUGAR COOKIE DECORATING KIT

I start bleeding green, red, and gold as soon as the wishbone has been broken and the leftovers from our Thanksgiving meal are packaged away in reusable containers. The spirit of the season just gushes out my body. The only bummer is that December seems to fly by each year, even when we try our hardest to slow it down and savor every moment. December 1 turns into December 24 in a wink.

I grew up baking with my mom and sisters for every holiday—especially for Christmas. We would spend the entire day making an assortment of cookies from around the world and deliver platefuls to friends and neighbors. So many memories are conjured up now when I measure, sift, and smell ingredients this time of year.

I wanted to continue this love of baking with my own children, so we began making Sugar Cookie Decorating Kits to deliver to friends in order to ease their burdens of the hustle and bustle this time of year. Our friends can find the joy in decorating cookies as a family without doing the dirty work—no messes of flour dust-clouds floating about the kitchen or scraps of dough remaining on the countertops.

To make it a fun event, we invite some of the kids' friends for a cookie-making party. We carefully roll out and cut dough with cookie cutters in all shapes and sizes: Christmas trees, gingerbread men, stars, and candy canes. We create kits with sugar cookies tied together with baker's twine, homemade buttercream frosting in small Weck jars, and bottles of festive sprinkles, then we deliver the kits to families with young children a few days before Christmas Eve in hopes that they will have a few cookies left to leave out for Santa Claus.

This is such a small and fun act, but I know it makes a huge difference in the lives of the young mothers who are trying their best to make memories with their small children. And we get the bonus of eating the leftover sugar cookies back at home.

SUGAR COOKIES

INGREDIENTS

FOR THE COOKIES:
- 1 pound butter (4 sticks)
- 2 cups sugar
- 2 eggs
- 1 tablespoon vanilla extract
- ¼ teaspoon almond extract
- 6 cups all-purpose flour, plus extra for dusting
- 1 teaspoon salt
- 1 teaspoon baking soda dissolved in 3 tablespoons milk

FOR THE FROSTING:
- 1 cup butter, softened
- 4 ½ cups powdered sugar
- ¼ cup milk
- ½ teaspoon vanilla extract
- ¼ teaspoon almond extract

DIRECTIONS

FOR THE COOKIES:
1. Preheat the oven to 350 degrees.
2. Combine butter and sugar until creamy.
3. Add egg, vanilla, and almond extracts; mix well.
4. In a separate bowl, combine flour and salt.
5. Add to butter mixture; mix well.
6. Slowly add baking soda/milk mixture to dough. Combine well.
7. Form two flat disks out of dough and wrap in plastic wrap.
8. Chill for 10 minutes.
9. Roll dough out on a floured surface, about ½ inch thick.
10. Use cookie cutters to cut various shapes.
11. Bake 9–12 minutes, making sure not to overcook.

FOR THE FROSTING:
1. Mix butter, powdered sugar, and milk until smooth.
2. Add vanilla and almond extracts; beat well.

december

"Glory to God in
the highest, and on
earth peace, good
will toward men."

LUKE 2:14

extra traditions

HERE ARE A FEW OTHER FAVORITE THINGS WE DO IN DECEMBER

CHRISTMAS COUNTDOWN

Make a Christmas Countdown. Get out the calendar and write out all of the activities you want to do during the holiday season (make snowflake quesadillas, go Christmas caroling, watch a Christmas movie, work at a soup kitchen). Fill an Advent calendar with activities each day leading up to Christmas.

DESIGN YOUR OWN WRAPPING PAPER

Roll out white craft paper and invite your kids to paint, color, or stamp their own designs to use for wrapping paper.

HOST A LIÈGE WAFFLE PARTY

Invite friends over to enjoy the yeast-laden, pearl sugar–coated waffles. Slather with Speculoos Cookie Butter, vanilla ice cream, homemade whipped cream, and fresh strawberries. I love treating my friends and family to these on my birthday in December.

COUSIN GIFT EXCHANGE

Have cousins choose names out of a hat to exchange gifts. Last year our kids and their cousins picked out hats for each other, and the year before they bought each other socks that fit their individual personalities.

HOMEMADE CINNAMON ROLLS

On Christmas morning, enjoy my sister's cinnamon rolls found on page 12.

TREASURED TEAM

ALEXIS ANDRA

STYLIST
EXTRAORDINAIRE

ALLY BURNETTE

PHOTOGRAPHER
(JANUARY, MAY, JUNE,
JULY, AUGUST, AND
NOVEMBER CHAPTERS)

KAYLA PLOUFFE

PHOTOGRAPHER
(FEBRUARY, APRIL, AND
OCTOBER CHAPTERS)

AMBER THRANE

PHOTOGRAPHER
(MARCH, JUNE, JULY,
SEPTEMBER,
NOVEMBER, AND
DECEMBER CHAPTERS)

KIMBERLY
ANDERSON
BLOIS

THE DAINTY LION
FLORAL ARTIST

KAYLA ADAMS

MASTERFUL LAYOUT
AND DESIGN DUO

JENN SANCHEZ

FLORAL ARTIST

NATALIE GILL

THE NATIVE POPPY
FLORAL ARTIST

LAURA ZATS

WISE INK
CONTRIBUTOR

PATRICK MALONEY

WISE INK
CONTRIBUTOR

ROSEANNE CHENG

WISE INK
CONTRIBUTOR

GRAHAM WARNKEN

WISE INK
CONTRIBUTOR

acknowledgments

I have an adorable quote from Roald Dahl framed in our craft room that reads, "If you have good thoughts, they will shine out of your face like sunbeams and you will always look lovely." Right now, I want to trade the word "thoughts" for the word "friends," because the friends and family I am about to address below have been sunbeams to me, and they make me feel lovely, inside and out!

Thank you to my Treasured Team, especially Alexis Andra and Kayla Adams. You have visually made this book better than I ever could have imagined. Alexis, I will treasure the downtime moments, sitting around the table munching on the leftovers from photo shoots with music humming in the background. Thank you for sharing your gorgeous home with me, along with props and out-of-the-box ideas. I will forever love the pile of cheese you created, fit for a king.

Thank you, Mom, for creating a meaningful environment in our home growing up. I anticipated every holiday because of you. We pulled out boxes of decorations together, baked together, and made everlasting memories, and we continue to make them together. Your love of life is infectious, and I am so lucky that our children get to experience it. Thank you for being involved in their lives.

Thank you, Dad, for your unwavering advice and support, for packing us kids up for an adventure around the world when I was only eleven years old, before cell phones, before drones, and before GPS. Thank you for the memories in the San Juan Islands with the illegal firework celebrations during the Fourth of July.

Thank you to my siblings: Jessica, Jenny, and Jamin. My life has been undeniably enhanced with all of you in it. I have learned so many life lessons from being the baby of the family. Jessica, thank you for sharing your love of baking with me and for sharing scriptures with me during times of trial. Jenny, I miss you more than words can ever express. You have taught me how to love unconditionally, without judgment (although I am still working on it), and I always admired you for sitting with your legs out-stretched on the floor playing with your kids even if laundry piled up and dishes were looming in the sink.

Jamin, thank you for being a rock, always. You are always there for me no matter what, and you put family first. Growing up with three sisters, you have definitely learned how to treat a woman, and Andrea is lucky to have you.

Also a huge thank you to so many other family members who have celebrated this life with me, in no particular order: Nana. My stepfather Alexx. Misha. Stepsiblings: Jennifer and Noah. Brother-in-law Darin and sister-in-law Andrea. Cousins: Jodi, Jaromy, Joanne, and Scott. Aunts and

Uncles: Gary, Pauline, Al, Cindy, Tony, Mike, Toni, Judy, Karen, Ron, Doreen, John, and Jeff.

To my husband's grandma, siblings and spouses: MaryAnne, Greg, Michelle, Peter, Kelsi, Kellie, Scott, and Brimley, and especially my in-laws Danny and Nanette. Thank you for sharing your traditions, and adopting some of mine. Thank you for Hawaiian Breakfasts, Little Italy on Christmas Eve, and X-mas Games. Our kids will remember them forever.

Thank you to my nephews and nieces: Zander, Trazer, Brix, Irik, Rastin, Kyde, Spree, Match, Wavy, Maya, Sage, Isla, King, Zara, Bear, Eden, Graham, and River, for letting me treat you like my own children with hugs and kisses.

Thank you to Ashley, Chelsea, Christy, Cora, Erin, Holli, Lindsay, Marie, Michelle, and Shellie, my book club friends who have kindled my love for holding good books in my hands and flipping through beautiful words and stories. I love our late night chats until one o'clock in the morning where we talk more about each other's lives than the books, but I wouldn't have it any other way. Thank you to my friend Jill who shows more confidence and interest in me than I deserve, and thank you for humoring me during our Solstice photo shoot.

Dylan, you are my true love. I cannot imagine life without you. Thank you for supporting me on this project, especially on the days where I wanted to quit. I love you more today than the day I married you, and you are my very best friend in all the world. Thank you for giving me our four treasures.

And to my four treasures: Seven, Shade, Melrose, and Gia. I do this all for you. Thank you for going with the flow during our photo shoots, and wearing the clothes that I laid out for you. Thank you for being flexible, and thank you for begging me to stop at Kentucky Fried Chicken on a long drive home from an all-day photo shoot where we had to make a detour to drop off rentals way out of the way. Stuffing those biscuits into our mouths is a memory with you that I will treasure forever.

ABOUT THE AUTHOR

Jaryn Jannard McGrath was born and raised in Southern California.
She studied at Brigham Young University, where she met her
husband, Dylan. Dylan and Jaryn have four children and a Maltese
puppy. They reside in North County San Diego.

Treasured Times is Jaryn's first book.